The Rights of Women Lesbian Custody Group was formed in 1982 to campaign and research around the difficulties lesbian mothers face in retaining custody of their children. The group consists of lesbian mothers and lesbian/feminist legal workers. The project offers advice and information, publishes articles, gives talks and organises workshops on issues related to lesbian mothers and child custody.

Lesbian Mothers' Legal Handbook was written by Markie Barratt, Varda Bondy, Gill Butler, Eve Featherstone, Pauline Gooderson, Lynne Harne, Carolyn Taylor and Fiona Watson. It was researched by Lynne Harne. Part One was edited by Markie Barratt, Part Two was edited by Lynne Harne.

Rights of Women Lesbian Custody Group
52–4 Featherstone Street, London EC1
Telephone: 01 251 6576

RIGHTS OF WOMEN
LESBIAN CUSTODY GROUP

Lesbian Mothers' Legal Handbook

The Women's Press Handbook Series

First published by The Women's Press Limited 1986
A member of the Namara Group
34–5 Great Sutton Street, London EC1V 0DX

British Library Cataloguing in Publication Data

Lesbian mothers' legal handbook.
   1. Custody of children–England 2. Lesbian
   mothers–Legal status, laws, etc. – England
   I. Rights of Women. *Lesbian Custody Group*
   344.2061'7   KD772

   ISBN 0–7043–3988–9

   Typeset by MC Typeset Limited
   Reproduced, printed and bound in Great Britain by
   Hazell Watson & Viney Limited,
   Member of the BPCC Group,
   Aylesbury, Bucks

Contents

To lesbian mothers everywhere

Acknowledgments

We would like to thank the following:

Action for Lesbian Parents, Valerie Cook, Sarah Forster, Pauline Fowler, Marion McAlpine, Nicky Mooney, The North London Lesbian Mothers Group, Sue Williscroft and Elizabeth Woodcraft.

The Lesbian Rights Project, San Francisco, California, for contributing information on American cases, and Chief Justice Elizabeth Evatt for information on Australian cases.

We would also like to thank Sue Beasley, Lyn May and Glynnis Nelsen for their illustrations, and the GLC Women's Committee for funding the project and the report *Lesbian Mothers on Trial*.

We would like to acknowledge all the lesbian mothers who took part in the survey that The Lesbian Custody Group carried out in 1984, and all those lesbian mothers who are unable to come out as lesbians for fear of losing their jobs or custody of their children.

Introduction

Many lesbians have children. Some lesbians have children through artificial insemination or a casual relationship with a man, but many have them during marriage or in a heterosexual relationship. When the relationship breaks up, there may be a legal dispute between the parents over who should have custody of the children. In the case of a heterosexual mother this usually presents no problem; the courts still assume, unless there are what it would regard as 'exceptional' circumstances, that the children should be with their mother. This applies particularly to younger children. But a mother's lesbianism immediately places her in the 'exceptional' category. The court's assumptions are reversed and the lesbian mother is put on trial.

Divorce law regards lesbianism in itself as unreasonable behaviour and the burden shifts to the lesbian, particularly in custody disputes, to prove otherwise. Many lesbian mothers still lose custody of their children solely on the basis of their sexuality, regardless of their parenting abilities and material circumstances. Even if the children wish to stay with their mother and she has looked after them almost exclusively since they were born, the judgment still often goes against her.

Lesbian mothers can be personally devastated by the experience of going to court where many face nothing short of blatant injustice. A lesbian mother may find that her entire life is put on trial; her personal relationships, politics and whole personality can be scrutinised and attacked. She can be subjected to insulting comments and remarks from the judge and the father's lawyers with little recourse. The legal system seems determined to undermine her decision to live as a lesbian and independently of men.

Many people are genuinely shocked by this discrimination, but most are simply unaware that it happens. During the 1970s, attempts were

1

made by lesbians to raise the issue publicly and to launch a campaign to fight the discrimination lesbian mothers face. In 1982 the Rights of Women Lesbian Custody Group was formed in London to support this campaign. In 1983 a national conference was organised to look specifically at the way the law treats lesbian mothers. Many lesbian mothers, lesbians and lesbian legal workers attended. Soon after the conference, the Rights of Women Lesbian Custody Group obtained a grant from the Greater London Council to research into the legal position of lesbian mothers with a view to changing the law and attitudes generally. A working group consisting of lesbian mothers and lesbian/feminist legal workers liaises with lesbian mothers' groups and offers an advice and information service to all lesbian mothers with legal problems. The group has organised a number of training sessions for women legal workers and has provided speakers for groups of law students, social workers and probation officers who may be preparing court welfare reports. The members of this group have also written this book.

This book is in two parts. The first is a guide to the law and how to survive it; the second is the result of a survey of the experience of 36 lesbian mothers. The book is written for lesbian mothers who now, or in the future, could be involved in a dispute about the care of their children. It will also be invaluable to legal workers acting for lesbian mothers. We have attempted to offer both legal advice and good practical advice. The law is deliberately shrouded in mystery; we have attempted to demystify the process and the glossary at the back of the book should help with unfamiliar terms. The issue of custody cannot be seen in isolation from a woman's race and class. A woman's access to housing and money are affected by her race and class, and these are often crucial in a lesbian custody case.

We look at other issues that affect lesbian mothers and lesbians who wish to become mothers. These include: money, making a will, adoption and fostering, self-insemination, immigration and nationality, and police powers.

The second part of the book provides an historical background to the law relating to custody, and examines Court of Appeal decisions made between 1976 and 1983. It dismantles the myths and stereotypes used against lesbian mothers. There is a brief comparison with the law in

Lyn May

Australia and the USA and we conclude with suggestions for change. This was originally published in 1984 by Rights of Women, as a report entitled *Lesbian Mothers on Trial*.

Throughout this book we have tried to strike the right balance between optimism and reality. Not all lesbian mothers lose custody of their children but the statistics and the personal accounts of lesbians who have fought custody cases can make depressing reading. With the publication of this book there is now no excuse for sloppy legal representation of lesbian mothers. We suspect, however, that many lesbian mothers will continue to know more about how to present their case than their legal advisers. Good legal advice is essential but it is not enough in itself. It is not enough whilst lesbians continue to be tried by a male legal system which regards us as abnormal and perverted. It is not enough when we face a system that has already tried and found us guilty before we even set foot in the courtroom.

This book is a small contribution to what we hope will be a growing campaign to win justice for lesbian mothers.

PART ONE

1
Understanding Legal Procedures

In this chapter we begin by explaining the basic legal terms that you will come across in a custody dispute, and outline the various ways in which you could become involved in such a dispute. We set out the five grounds under which a divorce can be granted and then go on to explain the various legal procedures that you will encounter depending on your circumstances when the dispute over custody occurs. The last part of the chapter describes wardship proceedings, which is another way that the issue of custody can be raised; conciliation, which is an informal way of getting you and the father to reach an agreement; and care orders, whereby the responsibility for a child is taken away from her/his parents and given to the local authority.

LEGAL TERMS AND PROCEDURES

Custody, care and control

The courts in England, Wales and Northern Ireland distinguish between care and control i.e. the day-to-day care of a child, and custody i.e. the right to make major decisions in a child's life concerning matters such as schooling and health. However, generally we have used the term 'custody' to cover both custody and care and control unless otherwise specified.

Custody can be granted to one person (sole custody) or to both parents (joint custody). Joint custody means that both parents are involved in making the major decisions about a child's life. The general practice is either to award custody, care and control to one person or to make a joint custody order but to give one parent care and control. Until recently joint custody orders were awarded in about 5 per cent of cases. However, courts are beginning to use them more frequently, even in cases where the parents obviously do not get on.

Unlike the courts in England, Wales and Northern Ireland, the Scottish courts do not make a distinction between custody and care and control. Custody (i.e. day-to-day care) is awarded to one parent and the other parent will automatically have certain 'guardianship' rights such as the right to a say in the children's schooling.

Access

Access is the right of the non-custodial parent to see her/his child/ren. There are two types of access which the court can order: reasonable and defined. Reasonable access means that you and the father make your own arrangements (this can be done through your solicitors) and defined access means that the court will stipulate the times and possibly the place when/where it will happen. An example of defined access arrangements could be 'staying access' one weekend in three, half terms, and half the school holidays.

HOW YOU COULD BECOME INVOLVED IN A CUSTODY DISPUTE

There are various ways in which as a lesbian mother you could become involved in a custody dispute. If you are married and you apply for custody of the child/ren when you file for divorce, your husband may oppose it. If you are married but separated you may want to apply for custody. Alternatively your husband could apply for custody on the grounds that you are a lesbian. This could happen long after your divorce/separation. If you are not married you have automatic custody of your child/ren but the father can still apply for custody.

On divorce

You may start having a relationship with a woman while you are still married and living with your husband. Although you may think that your husband will be agreeable to divorce and your having the child/ren, in our experience many men apply for custody as a way of revenge.

> Sue had been married for nine years and had two children. She started having a relationship with a woman and when she applied for divorce and custody her husband decided to oppose custody solely on the grounds of her lesbianism.

After divorce

The question of custody is never closed however long the child/ren may have been living with you, so even if you were divorced several years ago, your ex-husband could still apply for custody.

> Jane had been divorced from her husband for five years when she had her first relationship with a woman. She lived in a small town and her ex-husband soon found out about it. Until then he had been seeing the child/ren about once a month and seemed quite happy about this arrangement. He had never mentioned that he wanted custody. However, as soon as he found out that Jane was having a lesbian relationship he went straight to see a solicitor.

Another possibility is that you got divorced some time ago, you have custody of the child/ren and your ex-husband has known about your lesbianism all along. Your ex-husband then remarries. There is another woman who could look after the child/ren and so he applies for custody.

> Kate's children had been living with her for four years when her ex-husband remarried and applied for custody. He won the case, but Kate appealed and was given custody after a long drawn out battle.

Custody when you are not married

If you are not married you automatically have sole custody of your child/ren. However, the father can still apply for custody and/or access.

Liz lived with her boyfriend and they had a daughter. When the daughter was three years old they split up and the boyfriend moved out. Liz had the day-to-day care of her daughter although she allowed her boyfriend to see her every weekend, but when he found out that Liz was having a relationship with a woman he applied for custody.

On separation if you are married

It is quite possible that you will find yourself involved in a custody dispute when you first separate from your husband and before divorce proceedings have begun. Your husband could apply either to the Magistrates'/County Court for custody or to the High Court for the children to be made wards of court. You could also do the same.

Glyn had been married for five years when she started having a relationship with a woman. Eventually she left her husband with her three-year-old son and moved in with her lover. The very next day her husband went to see a solicitor and applied for custody.

THE WELFARE PRINCIPLE

Since 1925 the major principle used in courts to decide who should have custody, care and control of a child in a contested custody case has been the *welfare principle*. This means that the 'welfare of the child' is treated as the major consideration in a custody dispute, and the wishes of the parents and other factors are considered to be of lesser importance. There are no legal guidelines laid down to say how the 'welfare of the child' shall be determined so the courts have complete discretion to decide what is 'in the best interests of the child' in each individual case.

Although there are no legal guidelines, judges have established some principles over the years which normally carry some weight in custody disputes. These are:

Young children should be with their mother

This is one of the most consistent principles in heterosexual custody cases. It is rarely kept to in lesbian custody cases.

Status quo

This means that a child who has been living for some time with one of her/his parents should not be moved and that her/his familiar environment should not be disturbed. It is almost the only factor which sometimes overrides a heterosexual mother's right to her child as the law stands at present. When it comes to a lesbian custody dispute however, the status quo principle is often disregarded, as is shown in our survey (see page 149).[1]

Physical requirements

This involves being able to satisfy a child's physical requirements i.e. health, accommodation and material needs. The amount of care and energy which can be given to a child is also taken into account.[2]

Keeping siblings together

Another principle is keeping brothers and sisters (siblings) together if possible and practical.[3]

Children's wishes

The wishes of the child/ren are considered but the younger the child, the less weight is given to her/his preference. In general, once a child reaches 10 or 11, some consideration will be given to her/his wishes, but the age varies depending on the judge. A child's wishes may be ascertained through a welfare report; or through the Official Solicitor in wardship proceedings (see page 68); or by the judge in private.

Sex of children

There is no consistent ruling based on the sex of the child.[4] Many heterosexual women have been awarded custody, without the presence of a father figure for their sons though the absence of a father figure has been used as a reason for denying a lesbian mother custody.

Conduct and character of the parties in relation to the upbringing of the child

A final principle, and one which appears to carry most weight in lesbian custody cases (but not in others) is the conduct of the parties. This must only be weighted in terms of how the conduct of the parties will affect the child's upbringing.[5]

In the past a wife's sexual behaviour, or the mere fact that she left her husband, was considered a factor to be taken into account when awarding custody. Now this is rarely the case except when the woman is a lesbian. The husband's adulterous or other behaviour never seems to have been considered relevant, except when he himself is a homosexual.[6] In so far as he is expected to provide a role model or a father-figure, this does not seem to involve much more than taking his son to a football match. In one case where custody was awarded to the father the judge was influenced by the fact that the son might eventually succeed to his father's business.[7]

PRECEDENTS

There are no absolute precedents in custody cases, though obviously cases in the higher courts (Court of Appeal and above) will carry more weight, and may be referred to in other cases. The judge has the power and discretion to consider each case on its individual merits and circumstances.

DIVORCE

There are five grounds on which you can divorce your husband or he can divorce you. The court has to be satisfied that the marriage has irretrievably broken down *and* either:

    1.   Your husband has committed adultery *and* you find it intolerable

to live with him

2. Your husband has behaved in such a way that you cannot reasonably be expected to live with him (otherwise known as unreasonable behaviour). If you have had or are having a lesbian relationship this is considered by the courts as unreasonable behaviour and a sufficient ground for divorce
3. Your husband has deserted you for two years
4. You have been separated for two years and your husband agrees to the divorce
5. You have lived apart for five years.

You can start divorce proceedings after you have been married one year. This is only relevant for grounds 1. and 2. as the other grounds relate to specific times.

CUSTODY DISPUTES

1. Within divorce proceedings

If there is a disagreement over custody of the children, within divorce proceedings, either parent can apply to the court to make the decision. The case will be heard either in the County Court, or in the Family Division of the High Court. In Scotland custody disputes are held in the two highest courts, the sheriff's and the Court of Session.

In divorce proceedings, even when you and your husband agree, a statement of arrangements for the children has to be made and put before the judge. This contains details about the children, such as who they are living with and which schools they attend. Very occasionally a judge can intervene and disagree with the arrangements. In the case of one of the mothers in our survey, a welfare report was ordered. Another mother who ultimately got custody of her children reported:

'My husband had agreed to me having custody, care and control, and him having good access. My husband knew that I was a lesbian, and when the judge heard about it, he tried to persuade my husband to have the children instead.'

Where there is disagreement the decision will be made by the judge, supposedly adhering to the 'welfare of the child' principle (see above). An interim custody application may be made before the divorce has gone through, to decide who the child/ren will live with in the immediate future before the full hearing. In certain areas of the country custody disputes are first referred to conciliation (see p. 15).

The divorce court also has the power to award custody to a third party. A relative or anyone else can apply for the court's leave to intervene and apply for custody or access once the proceedings have begun.

2. *On separation during marriage*

The Magistrates' Court can deal with custody disagreements where you and your husband have separated while still married. A custody hearing in a Magistrates' Court will be heard by three magistrates, one of whom has to be a woman. A Magistrates' Court can order a welfare report, and hear oral but not written evidence. No notice needs to be given of evidence to be used against the other side. Joint custody cannot be awarded in the Magistrates' Court. As in divorce proceedings the court does have the power to award custody to a third party, but that party has no right to intervene in the proceedings.

3. *Where you are not married*

If you are not married you automatically have sole custody, care and control of your child, *but* the father can apply for custody and/or access, either to the Magistrates' Court, the County Court or the High Court under the Guardianship of Minors Acts 1971 and 1973 (or he can apply for care and control in wardship proceedings). He has to be recognised as the father, and have some relationship with the child, in order for his application to be successful. His name does not have to be on the birth certificate. Custody proceedings then follow the same procedure as outlined earlier, depending on the court. A local authority can intervene and grandparents have the right to claim access.

4. Wardship proceedings

Another way you can be threatened with a custody dispute is through wardship proceedings. A vengeful father, the local authority or any other person can apply to have a child made a ward of court. Application is made to the Family Division of the High Court. Once a summons is issued the child automatically becomes a ward of court straight away. This means that the court makes all the decisions about the child's life. The Official Solicitor (see p. 68) may be asked to act for the child, and does so if the court considers the child old enough to have her/his own views. The child is then made party to the proceedings. The Official Solicitor conducts an investigation similar to that of the welfare officer, although a welfare report may be ordered as well. Under wardship proceedings the strict rules of evidence do not necessarily apply. Hearsay evidence may be admitted, the child may be interviewed in private by the judge, and in some cases reports may be received by the court but not disclosed to you and the father.

CONCILIATION

Conciliation aims to bring parents together to discuss their differences and encourages them to reach an agreement without going through a full court hearing. There are two main types of conciliation service: 'out-of-court' schemes and 'in-court' schemes.

'Out-of-court' schemes are often run by social workers and/or voluntary organisations and take clients who may not yet have started legal proceedings. You do not have to go through 'out-of-court' conciliation if you do not wish to.

However, most schemes are 'in-court' schemes. First you go before the Registrar with your solicitor and then you see the court welfare officer. If your child/ren are over 9 they will have to be there. In some courts you have to go to conciliation and in others you can refuse. Each court has its own procedure, for example some welfare officers will ask to see the parents together, and others will see them separately. There is no referral to conciliation in Scotland.

Beware of conciliation! The object of conciliation schemes is to get you and your husband to reach an agreement without going to court; there will therefore be pressure on you to agree. Don't agree to anything you are not absolutely certain about. You can continue with a court hearing if you want to.

CARE ORDERS

The divorce court has the power to make an order for a child to go into care if there are 'exceptional circumstances', which make it 'impracticable or undesirable for the child to be entrusted to either party to the marriage or any other individual'. As can be seen in the appeal case of Re P 1982 (see Chapter 12: Lesbian Mothers v the Courts) however, the courts are reluctant to take their aversion to lesbianism as far as this.

There are several ways a child can be taken into compulsory care. The two main ways are:

1. Under the Children and Young Persons Act 1969 the local authority has the power to apply to a Juvenile Court (Magistrates') to have the child taken into care. The Juvenile Court can make a care order if, among other things, the child's proper development is being 'avoidably prevented or neglected' or s/he is in 'moral danger' *and* the court is satisfied that the child is in need of care or control. At the court hearing both the parents and the child can be represented by a solicitor. Where there is a conflict between the child and the parents, the court may appoint a Guardian ad Litem (see Glossary) to represent the child. The Guardian ad Litem is chosen by the court from local panels of social workers. If the case is proved then the magistrates can make a care order or supervision order. There is a right of appeal to the Crown Court. Further, the local authority can apply immediately for a 'place of safety' order from a magistrate if it considers that there are such grounds for care proceedings as stated earlier, or if it has reasonable cause to suspect that the child has been assaulted, neglected, or ill-treated. Parents need not be informed about the application. If the order is granted your child will be taken immediately into the temporary care of the local authority. A place of safety order

can last only 28 days but during that time the local authority can apply for a care order.

2. Under The Child Care Act 1980 a child can be taken into care through a Parental Rights Resolution. The local authority has the power to pass such a resolution (without going to court) if the child has been in voluntary care for more than six months, and if certain conditions are fulfilled. One of these conditions is that the parent is 'of such habits or mode of life as to be unfit to have care of the child'. You have one month in which to object to the passing of a Parental Rights Resolution; and if you do, the local authority must bring the matter before a juvenile court. The court can order either that the resolution lapses, or that it remains in force. For the resolution to stay in force, the grounds for passing it must still apply, and it must be in the best interests of the child. Once passed it remains in force until the child is 18, unless it is rescinded by the court or an adoption order is made.

RIGHTS TO ACCESS WHEN A CHILD IS IN CARE

Once a child is in compulsory care the parent has no automatic right to access, but if access has been terminated by the local authority, a parent can appeal against the decision. The ROW lesbian custody group knows of a mother being refused access to her child on the grounds of lesbianism.

2
Precautionary Measures and Getting Support

In this chapter we discuss the precautions you might want to take depending on your particular circumstances and situation, and outline sources of support.

TO TELL OR NOT TO TELL

If you have not yet left the shared home and your husband/boyfriend does not know you are a lesbian then you will have to make a decision about whether to tell him. You may decide that you are not going to tell him at all, or that you will tell him after you have separated, or before or after the custody of the children has been sorted out. You may think you will have no problems over custody, but if you tell him his attitude towards you is likely to change. Once he knows you are a lesbian, he is likely to bring it up in custody proceedings and use it as a reason why you should not have the care of the children. You are also giving him grounds to divorce you for unreasonable behaviour i.e. your lesbianism (see Chapter 1). If your right to stay in this country is dependent on your husband's status then you need to be extra cautious and not give him ground to divorce you (see chapter on nationality).

You need to bear in mind that 99.9 per cent of men are not able to accept lesbianism. Even if your boyfriend/husband has expressed support for the lesbian and gay movements or for women's liberation, *when it comes to you and the children it will be different.* Even when you feel that you have had a close and understanding relationship with a man for many years it is still likely that he will feel extremely threatened by your lesbianism. He may want to take his revenge on you by applying for custody of the children, or by making life as difficult as possible. If you have decided not to tell him make sure that you do not leave any 'evidence' around, for example letters that could give him reason to suspect that you are a lesbian.

When we asked other lesbian mothers (who have been through custody disputes) what their advice would be some of them expressed the following views:

'Tell women they should never admit anything about a lesbian relationship unless they are prepared to fight and maybe lose a custody battle.'

'If I had known that lesbians are in danger of losing their children, I could have left my husband on the many other issues that there were between us.'

'Don't tell the husband/father, however anti-sexist he may appear. He will always use it against you. He will try to make you feel guilty about the children and about splitting up the family.'

Another reason not to tell him, at least until you have separated, is that he may become violent towards you, your lover or your lesbian friends. He may in this way force you to move out without the children, which may make it more difficult for you to fight for custody. He may also try and turn the children against you by insulting you, or abusing you in front of them. In a survey we did on the experience of lesbian mothers in custody disputes (see Chapter 14) four women had to leave home without the children because of their husbands' violence towards them once they discovered their wives were lesbians. Three women had to get ouster injunctions (see Glossary) to get the man out of the shared home because of his violence. Ten out of 36 lesbian mothers had experienced violence towards them or their lovers/friends in some form. A violent reaction from your husband/boyfriend is therefore a real possibility.

Some men are not able to accept that a relationship has ended, and resort to various forms of harassment or threats, violence or sexual abuse. In these circumstances your best strategy is to leave home and take the children with you. If you have been physically assaulted or sexually abused, or have been put under emotional strain, you could try for a place in a women's refuge, where you can stay safely with the children, and where you will get help to find other accommodation. (See Resources list for women's refuges.)

Coming out

If you have recently become a lesbian, you may feel very happy and positive about your identity, and want to tell everyone, including friends and relatives, as well as your husband/boyfriend. Again, you need to think carefully about who you tell, whether it could get back to the father and what the consequences could be. Some women found that when they have come out heterosexual friends or relatives have turned against them, and taken the father's side. In a few cases this has resulted in heterosexual women friends/relatives giving evidence against a lesbian mother in court.

One woman stated: 'I met with open hostility from family and friends and was treated as an unnatural woman.' Another woman from our survey said:

> 'I have been genuinely amazed by the obvious feeling from friends and acquaintances, that basically I asked for everything I got. Firstly by leaving home "for no good reason", and then for having a lesbian relationship – the reaction I got was "oh no wonder the poor man is in such a state". A reasonably close friend left her relationship (with a man) and went to live with my ex-husband, primarily out of concern for his general welfare. The week before she moved in with him he had put me and my lover through a window, when he bumped into us at a party.'

If you feel that you need to tell someone and you have no close lesbian friends you can trust, then phone up one of the lesbian lines where you will be able to talk to another lesbian/lesbian mother (see Resources).

You may decide that at some point you are going to have to tell the father that you are a lesbian. If you are living in a different area, or town, then you may think he will never find out. If, however, you have moved just up the street or nearby, then you need to consider carefully. Bear in mind that custody orders are never final, and that he could apply for a variation order on the grounds that he has found out you are a lesbian. If he did apply for custody in this way, he would not necessarily get it, but it is a possibility. The longer the children are living with you, the less likely the courts are to want to move them, but it can happen.

Sue Beasley

One woman who was living with her daughter for six years, lost custody when she started living with her lover and the father then decided that he wanted the child. Another father began custody proceedings when he saw the mother in a television programme about lesbians. He did however drop the case when he was advised he had little chance of getting custody, since he had not had much contact with the child for eight years.

You may decide that you do not want to live a life of secrecy, and that you do not wish to hide your lesbianism from your children. In this case you need to think about whether you are prepared to fight a custody battle and possibly lose custody.

If you do decide to tell the father, given it is likely that he will find out at some point, the best time to do it is after you have separated, when you have found alternative housing, and when you feel strong and have made some plans about your life.

IF YOU HAVE ALREADY TOLD HIM THAT YOU ARE A LESBIAN

If he already knows that you are a lesbian, it is not the end of the world, and in any case you might feel that he will have to know at some later date. Possibly your first strategy will be to try and persuade him to let you have custody of the children (if you are still on speaking terms). One woman achieved this by talking to her husband about it every night until he finally gave in!

You can also tell him that if he contests he will not necessarily win, and that more and more lesbian mothers are getting custody these days. Contesting custody will involve him in a lot of hassle, and often financial strain in terms of legal fees. You could also spell out just how much work it is bringing up children and what it will actually mean if he has total responsibility for them.

If none of this works you could try bargaining with him, but this is probably best done through a solicitor; in any case, at this stage, you may only want to talk to him through a solicitor. (See Chapter 4: Out of Court Strategies.)

Where he knows or suspects that you are a lesbian and you are still living in the same house, you need to consider what he could possibly use as evidence against you if it came to a court case. Some men have stolen private diaries and letters, others have used tape recordings of phone conversations, attendance at lesbian or feminist meetings, lesbian books, posters and leaflets. The courts have accepted this sort of evidence.

Whether you are still living in the shared home or not, you need to consider how public you want to be at least until the custody issue is settled, and whether your husband/boyfriend could use your openness as a lesbian or your 'political or social activity' against you in a court hearing.

IF YOU HAVE ALREADY MOVED OUT WITHOUT THE CHILDREN

You may have decided that you don't want custody of the child/ren. In this case you need to consider what you want in terms of access. (See access section.) If you still want to get custody, however, don't give up hope: you still have a chance of getting the children back. In this situation you must begin proceedings for custody as soon as possible, because the longer the child/ren are living with their father, the less likely the courts are to disturb the existing arrangement ('status quo').

There are several things you can do to show that you still care and are very much involved with the children. These include visiting them as much as possible, or having them to stay, keeping in touch with their progress at school or nursery, and keeping an eye on their health and general well being. A good idea is to keep a diary, and note down when you see your children, when your husband/boyfriend prevents you from seeing them, your visits to their school, and possible visits to the doctor. Make sure you return the children on time and keep to the arrangements. If you are extremely worried about their state of health, or you feel that they are being really neglected, you could think about involving your local social services. They might check up on the sort of care the father is giving them. This might also provide evidence in your favour, if it comes to the court deciding custody. However, the response you get will depend on the individual social worker and the policies of your local social services. You therefore need to act with caution.

WHAT TO TELL THE CHILDREN

What you tell your children, will depend very much on your circumstances, their ages and their ability to understand the situation.

If you are divorcing or breaking up with the father, it is as well to explain to them that the two of you no longer get on, and have decided to live separately.

If the father does not know you are a lesbian

After separation, if the children are living with you, you may feel that you are able to explain to older children that you are having a relationship with a woman but that if the father found out they might have to go and live with him, because of society's disapproval. Older child/ren of separated or divorced parents frequently do not discuss the private life of one parent with another parent because they understand that this could cause problems and rifts between parents that they themselves don't want. Your lesbianism will, however, give them an additional reason not to talk about your relationships. Younger children, however, may find it difficult to keep silent, and you need to decide what to do about this.

You may feel that you want to keep the fact that you are a lesbian totally from your children, or that they are not old enough to understand the way society discriminates against lesbians. This will depend very much on how you intend to live your life and whether you feel you can conceal your relationships from them until they are old enough to understand or old enough to leave home. However, even young children are aware of close relationships between adults and want some explanation about what is happening, particularly if there is a lover living in the same house.

One woman, who was divorced before she came out as a lesbian, said: 'My daughter's father doesn't know I'm a lesbian. I don't know what his attitude would be, and I'm not going to ask him, but the fear of what he could do controls a lot of my life and her life too. She goes to stay with him regularly and she has to keep a careful silence on our activities.' Another woman who had always denied her lesbianism to her ex-husband stated that she felt she had to stay 'firmly in the closet', to her two younger children who were between the ages of 4 and 6 as they were too young to keep silent, although she had tried to tell her older child. She feared her ex-husband would go for custody if he found out about her lesbianism. She felt however, that it was a great strain to have to conceal such an important part of her life.

You may feel that to have to keep your lesbianism secret even from your children, is too heavy a price to pay and you would prefer to be able to live openly. These are questions only you can work out for yourself, together with friends or your support group, and will depend on what you feel able to live with.

If the father already knows you are a lesbian

The courts' attitudes tend to vary on what the children should know, but one Appeal case went against the mother when she said that her little boy need not know about her lesbian relationship. (*E v E* 1980.) The court felt concealment would not be possible for long. However, the courts do not like you to 'flaunt' your relationship in front of the children, and would expect you to be 'discreet'. This can mean anything from not living with a lover, to not kissing and cuddling in front of children or not telling them specifically that you are a lesbian. The same is not expected of heterosexual behaviour of course, and this is one of the most blatant examples of heterosexism displayed by our judiciary. In some American cases the courts have ruled that children can cope better with hostile attitudes towards lesbians from the community if they are living with their lesbian mothers. (See Chapter 15: Lesbian Custody Cases in the USA.)

What you say to the children and what you expect them to take on, will again depend on their ages, their level of understanding, and those attitudes they have picked up from our heterosexist society. You may feel this is something you want to discuss with other lesbian mothers or friends. (See p. 27.)

SEPARATION AND YOUR IMMIGRATION POSITION

If you married a man who has limited leave to stay in the UK and you entered the UK as his dependant (i.e. he has to maintain/house you), your leave to stay in the UK will be limited to the same as his. If you separate (or divorce) and he stops maintaining/housing you, you won't be able to get your limited leave extended. Once it runs out you could be in danger of being deported (i.e. sent out of the UK). You may be able to stay in the UK in your own right, but you should get advice from a reliable agency (see Chapter 9).

SEPARATION AND HOUSING

You can try and get the man to move out of the home. If he will not go you yourself might have to move. If he has been violent towards you you could get an ouster injunction (see Glossary). However, if he knows you are a lesbian, he may well bring up your lesbianism in his defence, and you could also find the custody issue raised before you have prepared your case.

If you have to move, try your utmost to take the children with you. The courts tend to look less favourably on mothers who have left their children. If in the end you get care and control, you may be able to move back into the previously shared home, as the parent who gets the child/ren also usually gets the home (see p. 81). If you cannot move back into the previously shared home your local authority should house you permanently.

It is often very difficult for lesbian mothers to leave home, because of the problem of finding somewhere to live. You may be able to move in with your lover, or friends, or you may not have these options. Some housing associations may be able to help you and the National Council for One Parent Families has an advice service on housing for single mothers (see Resources list). Also if you and your husband/boyfriend have a joint tenancy some councils may rehouse you if the marriage has irretrievably broken down. If you have had to leave home because of the father's violence your local authority should either provide temporary accommodation for you and your children, or get you a place in a refuge for women leaving violent men (see Resources list). Try and get as decent accommodation as possible. If it comes to disputing custody through the courts the standard of accommodation you can provide for the children will be assessed since it is one of the factors that the courts take into consideration. You also have to weigh up whether to move in with a lover (if this is a possibility) and how this may be viewed by the courts if your lesbianism is known. It is almost impossible to say what the courts' attitude to this would be, as it varies a great deal.

If you can show that you are in a long-term stable relationship, and your lover is committed to bringing up the children with you, then the court may view this favourably. On the other hand it may think your lover is unsuitable, or that living with her will be a bad influence on the children. If you live with a lover and it comes to court hearings, she may also need to appear in court. If you live on your own, the courts may think this is better, because your relationship is not being continuously 'flaunted' in front of the children. However, they may also think you have unstable and impermanent relationships so it is difficult to win either way. The courts do not look favourably on communal households, so if you are likely to be involved in a custody battle you need to think carefully about this. If your husband/boyfriend does not know you are a lesbian, and you move out to live with your lover, or into a lesbian household, you must consider whether he could find out.

GETTING SUPPORT

If you are about to go through a custody or access dispute or you are thinking about how to sort out the arrangements for yourself and the children, it helps to have support. Even if you have a very sympathetic solicitor, she will often not have the time to give you the emotional support you need, or to help you reach decisions about what to do. A lesbian friend, or better still a group of friends, may be able to provide such support. One woman told us: 'When after living with my daughter for years I suddenly found myself involved in a custody case it was like a nightmare. I only managed to get through it with the help of my friends. I asked three of them to be a sort of informal support group, we had meetings to discuss my case and they also went with me to see my solicitor.' There are a number of lesbian mothers groups around the country, where you can get support and share your experience. However, most of these groups are in large cities. You can telephone your local Lesbian Line or London Lesbian line to find out if there is such a group near you (see Resources list). Some Lesbian Lines also have lesbian mothers working on the line who you can talk to.

It's important to remember that you are not alone, and that there are many thousands of lesbian mothers who have been through or are going through a similar experience, even if you do not know any close to where you live.

THE TIME FACTOR AND STRESS

A custody or access dispute can often take a long time to be resolved; in some situations it may take as long as two years. There may be a considerable lapse of time between solicitors exchanging correspondence, the filing of papers, court hearings and adjournments. You have to be prepared for this, and recognise that it may put stress on many areas of your life. Unfortunately the wheels of the law turn very slowly. One lesbian mother who has been through a custody dispute has written: 'Never underestimate the psychological and mental effects that it has on you. Try and get support from as many women as possible – it's very easy to feel isolated even if you live with a lover.' Another mother wrote:

'Find a support group of lesbian mothers who have been through it. Non-mothers don't really understand. If like me you decide to leave to prevent further aggravation, you need to talk to women who made the same decision, as the worst thing was self doubt about my worth as a mother.'

GUILT

Because you may be under attack from all sides, even from former heterosexual friends as well as your ex-husband or boyfriend, you may find that your self-confidence, your belief in yourself and your ability to mother are undermined. Many lesbian mothers have described how these attacks have made them feel guilty, anxious and depressed. But they have survived and often come out much stronger. A lesbian mother who went through a long-drawn-out custody battle and won says, 'You need to hang on to how strong you are, don't let them get you down, I constantly had to be reminding myself of this'. You must remember that the courts are focusing on your lesbianism, not becuse lesbians make bad mothers, but because you are stepping out of the role which has been defined for you by our male-dominated society, i.e. to be dependent on a man; to be there to service him, and bring up *his* children.

FRIENDSHIPS

Getting support from other lesbian mothers and lesbian friends has often been crucial in helping lesbian mothers to survive the difficult period of a custody battle whether they go to court or not. Friends can help you talk through the difficult decisions you may have to make and put a perspective on things. You may also need support in looking after the children whilst you are visiting solicitors, going for court hearings, or just feeling vulnerable and down. Getting support with childcare, or being able to share childcare with other lesbian mothers, is something that can make all our lives better.

FAMILY

Some lesbian mothers can get support from their families. Many, however, cannot and have often been rejected by parents and other relatives and dismayed by their adverse reactions. In some cases mothers or fathers have given evidence against their daughters in court. One woman who was involved in a custody dispute said 'My child's paternal grandmother started seeing her solicitor about getting care and control. She knew I was a lesbian . . . she also phoned my parents to persuade them that my child would be better off with her. She also told my mother that I was a lesbian.' You therefore need to be very cautious with your own family, particularly in what you tell them. There is an organisation called Parents' Enquiry which helps families to deal with their own prejudices (see Resources list.)

LOVERS

If you are about to go through a custody dispute, it can put great pressure on your current relationship. Your lover may feel threatened, or unable to give you the support you need. At some points it may seem that you are being asked to choose between her and the children. As one woman said:

> 'I was told by my legal representatives that I would have to choose between my lover and my child and might well lose them both. My lover became the scapegoat for everything and we became turned against each other so that we did not even have our mutual support and love to fall back on.'

Where possible it is probably better for both of you to try and get support outside the relationship.

Your lover will have to work out her relationship with the children, if any, independently from you. If it comes to a court case, the court will want to know about this relationship. The following statement from one woman is typical of many cases: 'My lover was not considered to be a "suitable parent substitute". Nobody ever considered whether she was intended or wanted to be a parent substitute anyway, or whether she maybe had a completely different role.'

RESOURCES

Women's Refuges

Women's Aid London office	01 251 6537
Women's Aid Northern office	061 228 1069
Scottish Women's Aid – Edinburgh	031 668 2949
– Glasgow	041 248 2989
Northern Ireland Women's Aid	0232 24904
Republic of Ireland	0001 961 002

Lesbian Line

To talk to another lesbian/lesbian mother, telephone London Lesbian Line, who will put you in touch with other Lesbian Lines and lesbian mothers' groups all over the UK.

London Lesbian Line   01 251 6911
Mondays and Fridays 2pm–10pm
Tuesday, Wednesday, Thursday 7pm–10pm

Lyn May

Action for Lesbian Parents

Gives advice by letter on lesbian custody.
Action for Lesbian Parents
c/o The Corner Bookshop
162 Woodhouse Lane
Leeds LS2 9HB.

National Council for One Parent Families

Has an advice service on housing for single mothers.
National Council for One Parent Families
255 Kentish Town Road
London NW5
Tel: 01 267 1361

Parents' Enquiry

Is an organisation which helps families deal with their own prejudices
against lesbians and gay men. For the address/telephone number
telephone Gay Switchboard 01 837 7324.

G A Neslen

3
Finding and Coping with Your Solicitor

HOW TO FIND A SYMPATHETIC SOLICITOR

Probably the best way to find a sympathetic solicitor is to be recommended one by other lesbian mothers who have been through custody cases. At least you then know that the solicitor is familiar with the main issues. However, no two cases are the same so do not expect her to have all the answers. You could be recommended one by a trustworthy organisation; in particular we suggest Rights of Women, Lesbian Line and Action for Lesbian Parents (see Resources list). There *are* some black and lesbian and/or feminist solicitors. One woman said of her solicitor: 'She was very sympathetic and understanding, probably because she had worked in close contact with women's organisations before, and had actually encountered lesbians before.' Whatever you do, do not just go into the nearest solicitor's office on the High Street: solicitors are as biased and prejudiced as anyone else. Another woman said that her solicitor 'told me that as things were in this country at present I hadn't a hope in hell of gaining custody. He was not interested in the quality of my mothering or my husband's poor relationship with the children.'

Making sure she is suitable

Even when you have been referred to a sympathetic solicitor you may still want to make sure she is suitable. You could first of all talk to her on the telephone, and you could take a friend along with you on your first meeting (and subsequent meetings).

33

At the first meeting you should outline your circumstances and make sure you feel confident that she has some committment to dealing with your case. Make it clear that you want to discuss all the strategies and want to take an active part in the case. Another woman in our survey said: 'I stated how I wanted the situation to be . . . and she accepted my choice. (She was) excellent, I can't praise the solicitor and firm too highly.' Let her know that if she is not prepared to work in this way you would rather she said so now to give you a chance to find someone else.

Things to check with her

Whether you are eligible for initial advice under the Advice and Assistance Green Form Scheme and/or Legal Aid (see Legal Aid section in this chapter). You should do this on the telephone when you make your appointment, otherwise if you do not qualify you will be charged an hourly rate which could be around £75 an hour.

Whether she has experience in 'Family' law/whether she has done any other lesbian custody cases.

That she herself does not have any doubts about lesbianism and lesbians raising children.

Whether she is familiar with the different strategies of a lesbian custody case (see Chapter 5 on In Court Strategies).

Whether she is aware of the arguments that may be used against you.

Whether she knows the importance of expert witnesses/research.

Whether she is prepared to accept help from a support group.

When is the most convenient time to contact her.

Whether she will be doing all the work herself, or whether she has an assistant.

Whether she is aware of racism and how it might affect your case.

How long she expects the case to last.

Dealing with your solicitor

Don't just sit back and say 'my solicitor is dealing with it'. If you keep in regular contact with her she is more likely to keep your file at the top of her pile and to keep up to date with it. However, solicitors do not like being harassed and it is important to keep a good working relationship with her.

Even if your solicitor is sympathetic, she may not have had much experience of lesbian custody cases, so you may have to do some of the work yourself, in particular the parts which are not strictly legal, such as finding out who may be the best expert witness.

The majority of solicitors are white and middle class and they tend to use a fair amount of legal jargon. Try not to be intimidated by this. It may be helpful to remember that the solicitor is meant to be working *for you*, so do not be afraid to ask her to explain something which you do not understand, or to challenge her on something with which you do not agree. If in doubt, ask her to send you a letter explaining it.

Coming out to your solicitor

Whether or not you come out as a lesbian to your solicitor depends partly on whether your sexuality is going to be an issue in your case: if it is, then obviously your solicitor must know at the beginning so she is aware of the kind of case she is dealing with. However, if you think the father does not know you are lesbian, or you are hoping he does not bring the subject up, or you intend to deny it, then you have to decide whether to tell her. You may feel you would rather be open with her. However, she is under a duty not to lie, so if you come out to her she cannot then deny that you are a lesbian if the issue is raised by the other side (see Chapter 5 on In Court Strategies).

Changing solicitors

If you are not altogether happy with your solicitor you can change to another one whether or not you are on Legal Aid. If you are on Legal Aid your new solicitor will request permission from the Law Society for you to change. It is important to find a new solicitor before sacking

your old one; something important might come up while you are
between solicitors.

YOUR BARRISTER

If the case is disputed in court, it is usual for a barrister to represent
you. It is the solicitor who instructs the barrister; however, you should
discuss with your solicitor which barrister it will be. There *are* a few
black, lesbian and/or feminist barristers.

A woman barrister

As a matter of strategy your solicitor may suggest that you have a male
barrister; the law and the courts are a bastion of patriarchy so there is
an argument for having a man on your side. However, probably the
most important thing is that you feel as comfortable as possible with
your solicitor and barrister and can trust them to do as you want and
this is far more likely if they are feminists.

Meeting your barrister

Your meeting with your barrister is called a conference. It will take
place in her office (chambers) and your solicitor will be there too.
Make sure you have a conference with your barrister at an early stage
so you can iron out any problems and discuss what evidence you will
need. You can bring up any points you feel strongly about, and if you
do not feel happy with the barrister you have time to change to another
one.

However, do not be put off your barrister if she seems to grill you;
this is a strategy to see how you will react in the witness box. Tell your
barrister that you want to choose the way your case is run and do not
be intimidated by her.

The barrister may try to pressurise you into compromising; be aware
of what she is asking you to do and the consequences and practicalities.
For instance, you may be asked to agree that your children do not meet
your lover. Tell her that you want to think about it; you can then
discuss it with your friends and/or support group.

SUGGESTIONS

Keep a folder/file with all your solicitor's letters; letters from the father; anything else relevant.

Keep a diary of events – solicitors like to know precise dates, whereabouts, witnesses etc.

Go through your folder/file regularly so you know what is going on, and exactly how far things have got.

Keep in regular contact with your solicitor.

When you ring her be ready with questions you want to ask her. Write things down before you ring her so you don't forget anything.

If there is anything you don't understand ask her to explain.

Always remember it is your case, do what *you* want to do.

LEGAL AID

Legal Aid is a scheme whereby, depending on your income, you can get financial help towards your legal costs. In some cases it may cover the whole of your legal fees.

Legal advice and assistance (Green Form Scheme)

Your first meeting with your solicitor and any letters she writes at the beginning of your case may be covered by the Legal Advice and Assistance Scheme, otherwise known as 'the Green Form Scheme'. Your solicitor can work out at your first meeting whether you are eligible and this will depend on your savings, your income and your outgoings. If you are on Supplementary Benefit or Family Income Supplement you will not have to pay anything. If you are on a low to medium wage you may have to pay a small contribution.

The Green Form Scheme only covers a small amount of work, so if there is more work to be done or your case looks as if it may go to court you will have to apply for Legal Aid. Again, depending on your savings, income and outgoings, you may have to pay a contribution. You may well qualify for Legal Aid even if you did not qualify for Green Form Assistance as the criteria are different. You should let your solicitor know if your income or savings change at any time.

It can take from 6 to 12 weeks for your Legal Aid application to be assessed. A Legal Aid certificate cannot be backdated. However, while you are waiting for it your solicitor should be able to carry on working for you under the Green Form Scheme. If your case is an emergency then there is a system whereby Legal Aid can be granted within a few days, or in some cases, over the telephone.

The statutory charge

If you have been granted Legal Aid and any property or money is 'recovered or preserved' in the proceedings i.e. if you have retained or been given property/money, the Law Society may be entitled to recover the costs it has incurred in the following ways:

1. If the former shared home has been in dispute and it is sold, the Law Society will take their costs from your share of the proceeds of sale. The first £2,500 is exempt. If the house/flat is not being sold immediately the Law Society will have a charge over it and will recoup their costs if and when it is eventually sold.

2. If you have been granted a lump sum of money, the first £2,500 is exempt but the Law Society can recoup their costs from anything above that. Any maintenance you receive is exempt from the Statutory Charge.

It may be possible to bring the dispute over custody and the dispute over the house under different court proceedings so that the costs of the custody case will not be affected by the Statutory Charge. Ask your solicitor about this.

Lyn May

RESOURCES

Rights of Women Lesbian Custody Group, 52/54 Featherstone St, London EC1, Tel: 01 251 6576.

London Lesbian Line, 01 251 6911, Mon to Fri 2–10pm, Tues, Weds and Thurs 7–10pm.

Action for Lesbian Parents, c/o The Corner Bookshop, 162 Woodhouse Lane, Leeds LS2 9HB.

4
Out of Court Strategies

Once you know you are going to be involved in a lesbian custody dispute, and you have found a suitable solicitor, there are a number of strategies you can adopt to try and keep the case out of court, and eventually come to some agreement. You may want to do this for a number of reasons. One is that if your case goes to court you will be up against the particular prejudice of the judge hearing the case. You may also be up against a prejudiced court welfare officer. Another is that custody hearings can be expensive, and even though you may well qualify for Legal Aid, you could have to pay this back if you get any money and/or property apart from maintenance out of the proceedings.

However, negotiations out of court, which are conducted through solicitors' letters, may take some time and could come to nothing. You may end up going to court anyway. Out of court negotiations can be very draining, and you may wish you had gone straight for a court hearing to get the issues settled one way or another. You also need to bear in mind that the father's determination to get the children may decrease over time, once he recognises what having responsibility for them means. One mother in the survey who went to court and lost advises women 'try as hard as possible to persuade the husband/father to drop the case and let you have the children'.

The following are a number of factors you may be prepared to bargain over through your solicitor.

MAINTENANCE

If you feel able to be self-sufficient, and think that you can raise the children without any maintenance from the father, then this could be enough to stop him contesting custody. There may also be property he wants which you can bargain over. Many men's egos lie in their pockets, and the fact that he won't have to pay for you to bring up the children, could decrease his resentment. One woman says: 'I purposely did not ask for maintenance for the children so as to avoid further acrimony.' Another says: 'It was after I started trying to get money out of him that he went to court for custody.'

ACCESS

Your husband/boyfriend may be content with an offer of frequent access to the children such as seeing them every weekend, and some of the school holidays. However, you must think whether you could stand this, and whether it would give him the opportunity to harass you and interfere with your life.

JOINT CUSTODY

He might agree to joint custody and let you have care and control. There are already moves by the Booth Committee (a committee set up under the Lord Chancellor's Office to look at matrimonial procedure) to recommend that joint custody is the usual order unless one of the parties objects. This may mean that lesbian mothers are in a weaker position to push for sole custody. It is unclear what joint custody actually means legally. But it can mean that the parent without care and control is involved in making major decisions in a child's life e.g. what school s/he goes to, whether the child should have a major operation etc. Even where one parent has sole custody, the 'non-custodial parent' has some rights to request school reports, and to attend the school. Joint custody can mean that the father thinks he has more rights to interfere in your life and your children's lives. So again, you need to think carefully about whether you can put up with this.

Several women in our survey said that they had had problems over joint custody. One woman said about the sort of control the father had over her: 'It is as simple and terrible as not being free. I am not able to be as honest and open with my child, my friends or my acquaintances about my life.' And another mother said: 'It's totally meaningless for women. Much like being married it means you do all the work and he takes the major decisions.'

It could mean that you will be unable to move your children to another school, or to move house. You could end up with a joint custody order being imposed by the court. Any such conditions can be made part of the order.

SHARED CARE AND CONTROL

This means that both parents share the care and control of the children half the time, e.g. the children stay one week with you and one week with their father or 3½ days with each of you. In practice it is frequently unworkable. It is difficult for the children and is not a strategy we would recommend. Children may feel totally confused by their different parents' lifestyles, and the father may use his time with the children to turn them against their mother. Some lesbian mothers have made these arrangements after separation to avoid going to court. At present shared care and control is an unusual order, but it may become more acceptable.

SPLITTING UP THE CHILDREN

If you have two or more children, one possible arrangement, which a few lesbian mothers have managed, is for each parent to have one child. This may work if the children are old enough to decide who they want to live with. However, the children themselves may not want to live separately and this has to be taken into account. The courts in general do not like to split up children. You yourself may feel that you want to live with both children, and you will have to think about whether you can cope with being separated from your other child/ren, and also whether they will be able to cope with being separated from you, and their sister/brother.

THE FATHER'S UNSUITABILITY

If the father is determined to use your lesbianism as a reason why you should not have custody, you need to consider whether there is anything the court would find unsuitable in his character or behaviour. If there is, you should make it clear to him via your solicitor that you will bring this up. He would be less likely to get custody if he has any convictions for sexual assault or abuse. Any convictions of a criminal nature could also count against him. Violence towards the children would also count (although not necessarily violence towards you). There may be other aspects of his character or behaviour that would be considered unsuitable, e.g. mental illness and possibly political activities. One father worked as a pornographic photographer in his own home, and the court considered this an unsuitable environment for the children. You should have no qualms about bringing up his unsuitability. He is using society's prejudice and disapproval of lesbianism to get at you and take away your children; if you are going to get custody then one part of your strategy may be to beat him at his own game. Unfortunately, in this situation you cannot afford to be principled, since the choice is not yours.

Finally, your determination to fight for custody even if it ends up in a court battle may be enough to encourage him to withdraw, particularly if you don't give in to threats and harassment. Many fathers do give up fighting for custody because, when it comes down to it, it's revenge they want, not the children.

TIMING

The Court will often award custody to a husband/boyfriend who has (re)married because it regards the heterosexual nuclear family as the best context for the bringing up of children. The fact that the children may be brought up by a step-mother with whom they have had little previous contact does not seem to trouble the courts. So it may be to your advantage if your custody case is heard before the father has remarried or started to live with another woman. Although in general the court does not like to move child/ren from their familiar environment (status quo), in lesbian custody cases this principle has been overruled where there has been the alternative of a heterosexual nuclear family.

As one woman reported:

'Although my daughter had been living with me for years, the court awarded custody to her father and his cohabitee because they could provide her with a home which was more "normal". The judge was very impressed by the cohabitee, who worked in one of the caring professions, and said that she would be a good influence on my daughter.'

CONSENT ORDERS (if you are married)

If you and the father do come to an agreement your solicitor will put it in writing and it then has to be approved by the court. ('Consent' custody orders cannot be made without one or both parties attending court. The judge has to be satisfied about the Order and even though you and the father may be in agreement the judge still has the power to change the order or refuse to make it in the terms of your application.)

In divorce procedure when the decree nisi is pronounced the judge has to be satisfied about the arrangements for the children and makes a declaration accordingly. If, for instance, the judge finds out that you are a lesbian, he may order a welfare report to be prepared or he could make a supervision order. If you are not taking legal proceedings but just separating, the agreement could be drawn up by a solicitor and would not need the approval of the court.

TAKING YOUR CHILD ABROAD

If you are married or separated/divorced and have joint custody, or if there is a Court Order which says that you must not remove your children from its jurisdiction you must get the appropriate consent before taking your children abroad, i.e. the consent either of the father or the court. If you do not get this agreement you will be committing a criminal offence and depending on the country where you are staying, the court may order you to return to the UK (Child Abduction Act 1984).

5
In Court Strategies

This chapter aims to give you information which you might need if you decide to go to court. It also tells you some of the things you can do to best prepare for your court case. The information is based on the experiences of women we know who have been through court cases themselves.

Going to court is always a risk, but as least if you and your legal advisers are well prepared, you stand a better chance of winning. Even if you lose – *a possibility you must always consider* – you will know that you did as much as possible under the circumstances to prepare your case.

The chapter covers various strategic considerations, such as which court to go to, if you have a choice; how to prepare for the visit or meeting with the court welfare officer; and what sort of issues might be raised by the welfare officer, by the father or by the other party's barrister in court. Legal procedure is often confusing and intimidating to the lay woman, so we have tried to outline some of the procedures involved, so that you know what to expect.

Although your solicitor should be aware of many of the issues that have to be considered, you need to do a lot of your own preparation and thinking about the most effective strategies to use. Your solicitor should follow your instructions on this, and discuss the strategies with you. You may know more than her, especially if you have read this book! So don't necessarily rely on her judgment.

GOING TO COURT

You may decide that you are not going to get the agreement you want, and in this case, you may be willing to fight it through the courts. If you decide you have to go to court, this should be your decision and not that of your legal adviser. If she does not agree then you will have to find another solicitor.

G A Neslen

CONSIDERATIONS

There are a number of things to take into account if you are considering a court battle. First, you need to think about cost. Although you may get Legal Aid, you have to bear in mind that you might still have to pay your own costs (see Statutory Charge in Legal Aid Section). One way of avoiding this would be to go for custody, before you get divorced, under the Guardianship of Minors Act. If, however, divorce proceedings have already begun you cannot do this. If you are not married, it is less likely that property matters will end up in court at the same time as custody. If they do the Statutory Charge may still apply.

Emotional strain and the time factor

It may take at least a year to go through a contested case, if not longer, although sometimes cases are heard quite quickly. You need to think whether you can stand the emotional strain of a long-drawn-out custody case. Of course if you spend several months trying to settle out of court, then this can also be very stressful.

Another strategic consideration is the wishes of the children, if they are old enough to be taken into account. If they are around 9 or 10 the court may be prepared to consider what they want. Whilst there are no hard and fast rules, and the court can go against the wishes of the children at times, if the children are determined that they want to live with their father, this may well be taken into account in the welfare report, and/or by the judge in private. In this case it would be much harder for you to convince the judge that it was in the children's best interest that they should live with you. Therefore it might be a waste of time going to court, unless you have a very good case as to why they should not live with their father. Where the children are determined that they want to live with you, this is obviously an advantage in a contested case.

Accommodation and money

If you have not already considered this you need to think about where you will live, if you can provide adequate accommodation, and also how you are going to provide for the children, because these are things the court will consider. For example will you be trying to get maintenance, will you be living on social security or will you be working? Unfortunately the courts still express double standards here. For instance, one woman said '(my husband) was thought very highly of for wanting to give up work to look after the children. I however was told that I must find work and cease to be a burden on the state.' In other cases the reverse is expected. If you are working you need to consider arrangements for the children whilst you are at work, or after school, as the court will want to know whether these are satisfactory. If you do not intend to move back or stay in the matrimonial or shared home, then you need to find suitable accommodation for you and the children. If you have no suitable accommodation, you can ask your solicitor to secure a letter from the Local Authority or Housing Association stating that they will house you if you are awarded custody. This letter should be attached to your affidavit (see below). If the children are of both sexes and over 10 they will need to have their own bedrooms. If you are intending to move to another area away from the children's present schools, then you need to think how the court will view this. It is not by any means inevitable that you will lose custody if you intend to move or have already moved with the children to another area, but depending on their ages and whether they are well settled in their present schools this is a factor that will be taken into consideration. You will have to produce some convincing arguments about the necessity to move.

WHICH COURT PROCEEDINGS?

Custody disputes can be decided in the Magistrates' Court, the County Court, or the Family Division of the High Court. Choosing your proceedings and which court you go to can be strategically important in winning your case.

Going to the Magistrates' Court

This will only be possible if you are just taking custody proceedings, rather than proceedings under divorce or separation. The Magistrates' Court can hear oral but not written evidence and there will be no notification of the evidence the father will bring against you. If the case is going to be a long one, with numerous witnesses on both sides, the magistrates may well refer it up to the County Court anyway. The magistrates will be either three lay people, one of whom has to be a woman, or one paid magistrate. It may be strategic to go to the Magistrates' Court if:
1. You think the father isn't very well prepared
2. You know the magistrates are fairly liberal
3. You need a quick decision

The main disadvantage is that you do not know the case against you in advance. *Most magistrates are not known for their liberal views.*

County Court

Most custody cases are heard in a county court before a judge. In divorce proceedings you can go to *any* (divorce) County Court. Your solicitor should have some idea of the views of various judges sitting in your area, and could possibly but not necessarily time your hearing to come up before a judge with more liberal views (if there are any). If all the judges are totally reactionary then you may want to consider getting the case moved to the family division of the High Court in London. However, you can only do this in certain circumstances and you need to get the approval of the County Court. Bear in mind that if the court refuses its permission you may have emphasised the lesbian issue more than you would have wanted.

Family division of the High Court

This court deals with complicated issues around custody and with wardship proceedings. The judges may actually have had some experience of lesbian custody issues. This does not necessarily mean they will be less prejudiced, or that you will get a fairer hearing, just because it is the High Court. You may get a County Court judge who is far less prejudiced than a High Court judge. High Court judges may be familiar with all the arguments that are used against a lesbian mother having custody. Moving a case to the family division of the High Court could be strategic, as a delaying tactic, but also more costly.

PREPARING YOUR COURT CASE – AFFIDAVITS

In a contested custody case (except in a Magistrates' Court) there will be sworn statements (affidavits) from both parties indicating what arrangements they would make for the children and why they think the children should live with them rather than with the other party. If you are the one starting the custody proceedings you will have to file an affidavit first, in support of your application for custody. The father will then reply to it, and give comments on why he should have the children. You are entitled to reply to this. If he is the one starting the custody proceedings, then you will reply to his affidavit. There will also be affidavits from witnesses. You will have to discuss the content of your affidavits and your witnesses' affidavits very carefully with your solicitor (see below for points you need to cover). These affidavits and the welfare report will be sent to the father's solicitor. The welfare officer will also be at court (if you and your legal advisers think it is necessary) to answer questions on her/his report. Other reports, such as school and medical reports, will be attached to your affidavit.

PREPARING YOURSELF AND YOUR WITNESSES

It may help to go over what you are going to say with a friend. Your witnesses also need to be prepared for questions that may come up in cross-examination. If you have never been to a court before try and visit your local County Court beforehand so that you are not so intimidated by the courtroom atmosphere (you will not be able to see a family court in action as family cases are heard in private).

CLOTHES

However much you may resent it, you may well be judged by how you look. Obviously the smarter and more respectable you can look the better. This also includes your witnesses.

THE WELFARE REPORT

In nearly all contested custody disputes there will be a welfare report. This means that your circumstances and those of the father or other party will be investigated by a court welfare officer. (In a wardship case it may be the Official Solicitor. For wardship cases see later.)

The court welfare officer will draw up a report which you will be able to see before you go to court. The welfare officer is usually a probation officer with experience of custody cases; in some parts of the country it could be a local authority social worker. A probation officer will have had a social work training with further specialisation in probation work. Most social work training gives very traditional views on childrearing. Preparation for the interview with the welfare officer is therefore very important, if you want to make a favourable impression. Your welfare report is very significant in deciding your case; although the welfare officer doesn't have to make recommendations as to who your children should live with, she or he frequently does. The judge does not *have* to act on the recommendations of the report, but usually will.

SOCIAL WORKER'S DUE TOMORROW...

NO PROBLEM...JUST HIDE THE LEGO, AND WE'LL DIG OUT A DRESS AND A DOLL!

Sue Beasley

Which welfare officer

You can't choose your welfare officer, but she or he may be able to choose you. If you know any social workers or probation officers in your area, then let them know that your case is coming up, and they may be able to take it on. Court welfare work is usually farmed out by the senior probation officer to other probation officers. A probation officer could choose to take on your case, because they are interested in it or because it is part of their normal workload.

The ROW Lesbian Custody Group knows of sympathetic probation officers. There may be one in your area who could take your case. If you think that your probation officer is particularly prejudiced, then you could try complaining to the senior probation officer. Otherwise your barrister must challenge her/him in court. If the welfare report is unfavourable your solicitor should make sure that the welfare officer is there so that s/he can answer questions on it.

Preparing for your interview

In any case you may get a probation officer with fairly traditional views, so prepare carefully for the interview. The probation officer may interview you in your home and may want to talk to the children separately, depending on their ages, so you should also let your children know about the visit. Some divorce court probation services now take a conciliatory role and only interview in their offices with the whole 'family'. They will try and push you into coming to an agreement about the children. You should resist such an interview if it is not what you want, or if you feel it would serve no useful purpose. This should be done via your solicitor if possible. The welfare officer will be looking at your relationship with your children, the home you provide for them and your mothering abilities. S/he will probably also visit the children's school. It may be useful to show her/him your child/ren's school reports.

Things to consider for the interview in your home

1. Do I want to present a respectable image? If so think about clothes, posters on the wall or anything that might be considered to be 'influencing the child/ren'.

2. Think about clothes the children wear, toys they are playing with. Your probation officer may be into traditional stereotypes of what boys and girls should wear, toys they should play with, and the sort of role models they are getting.

3. Being a lesbian. Your probation officer may well have stereotypical and prejudiced views about you being a lesbian and *may assume* that this will adversely affect the children.

The welfare officer and the court will be considering similar issues in relation to your lesbianism. These are dealt with together below.

Various issues must be considered to do with your affidavit, your witnesses' affidavits, the welfare report and questions that may arise in court. In all cases you must think about how your situation can compare favourably with the father's situation:

– Accommodation – is it adequate?
– Finance – how are you going to provide for the children?
– Schooling and childcare
– Your mothering abilities
– Questions around your sexuality and how it affects the children

The first three are common in all custody cases but the last two may be related to your lesbianism. These will be dealt with more fully below.

YOUR MOTHERING ABILITIES

Prepare your state of mind. You may feel that your mothering is being put on trial. Remember that all mothers are made to feel that they are inadequate at sometime in their lives; this is part of the way we are controlled by men. The perfect mother does not exist. Reassure yourself that there is absolutely nothing wrong with your being a lesbian mother and that there is no reason why you should have to feel defensive about it. Your children are likely to get many benefits from growing up with you, benefits they would not get in the heterosexual family. Keep reminding yourself of this.

Your barrister should be familiar with the psychological evidence that shows there is no difference between lesbian mothers and heterosexual mothers bringing up children and should be prepared to argue it. (See end of the book for a summary of this evidence.) If necessary you should also call an expert witness to put the evidence (see Resources list).

Aspects of your mothering abilities may be questioned and linked with your lesbianism. It may be suggested that you do not care for the children properly, by taking them on demonstrations, or by 'dumping' them on other women, or, one extreme example, by letting them starve. It is important that you have witnesses who will refute such allegations, and who can vouch for your caring abilities and the children's wellbeing. Your own mother may be appropriate here if she will support you, or a neighbour who is a mother, and whose children have contact with your children, and possibly a health visitor or social worker. If you work you must show that you have made suitable arrangements for the children to be looked after while you work, or to be picked up from school. Even when you don't work you may need to show you have some support; (if, for example, you have to go into hospital).

QUESTIONS ABOUT YOUR SEXUALITY

If you are the person who has started custody proceedings you may not feel it is relevant to bring up your lesbianism in your first affidavit. If the father raises it in his affidavit then you have the right to reply. Even if it is not mentioned in the affidavits it may come out in court.

Where it has been raised, or you think it may be raised, you need to consider how you are going to deal with it. You should discuss this thoroughly with your solicitor, and insist on a conference with your barrister and your solicitor. You may not be prepared to answer offensive questions that are asked about your sexuality, and that are irrelevant to the welfare of your child/ren. Lesbian mothers have been asked what they do in bed, what they wear in bed, whether they have sex in front of the child/ren, whether they use appliances etc. For instance, one mother reported: 'Just about the only questions the Judge asked me in two days of court hearings were "Did my daughter see my lover and me in bed together? Did she know what we *did* in bed together? Did I want her to be a lesbian too?"' If you feel you do not want to answer such offensive questions this is your choice. You should instruct your barrister to object to such questions on the grounds that they are irrelevant to the welfare of the child/ren. You should feel absolutely certain that your barrister will carry this out forcibly, and not let you down. If s/he feels defensive about this and has doubts her/himself then you should get someone else. Your barrister should

PLEASE SIR CAN
I STAY WITH MUM,
I PROMISE I WON'T
BECOME A LESBIAN.

Lyn May

be familiar with previous cases where the mother's sexuality has only been considered as one factor among many, and where this hasn't prevented lesbian mothers getting custody[1] and you should make sure that s/he will present the case in this way. One woman in our survey said: 'The barrister was apologetic about our gayness. The focus of the case was our lesbianism and sexuality. Our willingness/ability to raise the children took a minor place in the hearing.' Another woman said: 'The thing is not to let them wear you down. Keep your self-respect. Keep your lesbianism in perspective as only *one* aspect of your life, and emphasise all the positive things you give your children.'

You also have to remember some of the myths judges believe about lesbians. The most common are that lesbians are 'oversexed', and that they seduce and molest children (see Chapter 13 on Myths). You may feel like challenging such myths in your affidavit. If they or any of the above questions are raised by the other side in court, you may think it is better to answer such questions, if it will help your case. There is no reason however why you or your lover (if she is going to be a witness) should be subjected to such a line of questioning. You need to expect such questions, and you and your barrister need to be prepared on the line you are going to take. You also need to be prepared for such questions that may come up in cross-examination. Expect the father's barrister to be as unpleasant as possible. The judge may also ask you unpleasant questions and can overrule objections. As the hearing is held in private the judge can conduct the proceedings on a fairly informal basis if s/he so chooses.

QUESTIONS ABOUT THE CHILD/REN

These issues may also be raised by the welfare officer, so you need to prepare what you are going to say before her/his visit. You may be asked what effect your being a lesbian will have on the children. The question could be phrased more generally, and you could be asked 'Don't you think the children will suffer?'.

Usually the court will not expect you to conceal your lesbianism from the children. A judgement went against a lesbian mother who claimed her child need never find out. (The Appeal of *E v E* 1980.)[2] It may be implied that the children will be unhappy when they find out you are a lesbian, because it is something 'unnatural', or 'deviant'. It is therefore best to take a positive approach. State that you have explained that you are a lesbian to the children, according to their ages and level of understanding (see section on Precautionary Measures). One way to approach this would be to say that you have told the children you love women, or your lover if you are in a particular relationship. You need to stress that there is nothing 'wrong' with this, but some people don't like lesbians and discriminate against them and you can show links with other forms of discrimination e.g. some people are discriminated against because they look different or have a disability. Therefore you should say that you have also explained to the children that it might not be something they would want to shout about at school or in the corner shop. They understand it is a question of other people's prejudices, and *not* that you are the problem. You might also want to state that being a lesbian is a positive choice, and that the prejudice that may be displayed by other people is not a reason for removing a child from its mother. Your children may be upset because you and their father have split up, on the other hand they could be happier. The probation officer may assume that they are upset because of your lesbianism. You need to stress that many children get upset at this time, particularly if they don't know who they are going to live with, and the future is uncertain.

'Would you want your child to grow up lesbian or gay?' This question is often asked. It is best to answer that your children would have a choice. As most parents have discovered, children cannot be forced into being anything they do not want to be. You could also make the point that most lesbians and gay men have heterosexual parents, so if the court is trying to suggest that you are forcing your children to be 'homosexual' this is irrational. If you say that you would prefer it if they were heterosexual, you may be laying traps for yourself, because you are by implication saying there is something 'wrong' with being lesbian or gay.

'Inappropriate models'

Questions may also arise about the so-called 'models' you are providing for your children, both in terms of your sexual relationships and what is regarded as appropriate behaviour for the different sexes. For example, it may be suggested that your children do not see heterosexual relationships, and that this is bad for them. The best answer to this type of question is that children are surrounded by heterosexual models and ways of relating. They get this from the media, on the street, in nurseries or schools, and from other children and adults. Psychological studies have shown that 'outside influences' have far more effect than any parental behaviour (see end of book for a list of these studies). It may also be suggested, particularly where the child is a boy, that he needs male role models. As one woman reported: 'They said my son would have a job to grow up "normal" without a male model permanently there to emulate.' Again male models and modes of behaviour exist everywhere we look; however, you could also produce some male witnesses to show that your child does have male adult heterosexual friends. Presumably your child's father will also have access, and this is another male role model. You could also stress that your children conform to what is considered the appropriate behaviour for girls and boys, but (if this is the case) that they also play non-specific gender games, and that you see this as positive.

Community disapproval

'Don't you think your children will be teased, suffer social stigmas, not be able to bring friends home if they live with you?' This question, phrased in various ways, may be asked or implied frequently. This is where you will want to produce witnesses such as neighbours, heterosexual mothers whose children play with your children, a school teacher or health worker if possible, male heterosexual friends (particularly if you have a boy) and members of your own family, if you have their support. You need to do this in order to show that your children are not isolated. You could point out that their relationship with you, and what they get from you, counteracts any discrimination. If you are sure that your family in particular and friends will be supportive and say the right things, then let the welfare officer know that they accept your lesbianism. This is where you and your legal advisors need to be familiar with the psychological studies which show that children living in lesbian households do not differ in their social relationships from children of heterosexual mothers and that they are not more unstable emotionally. (The studies are listed at the end of this book.)

You could stress that children get many positive benefits from living with lesbian mothers. There is no reason why your barrister should not quote American cases which are relevant to the issue of community disapproval, such as the case of Belmont v Belmont,[3] where the judge ruled that the children could cope better with hostile community attitudes if they continued to live with their mother. (For further information on these cases and where to get them see Chapter 15 on Lesbian Custody Cases in the USA and Further Reading and Information at the end of the book.)

Your relationship and effect on the children

A lover
If you have a lover whom you see on a regular basis or who lives with you, then the welfare officer and the court may be concerned about her relationship with the children, and you will have to discuss with her and your legal advisors whether she should appear as a witness. It may well be positive if she is willing to do so, especially if the father has made allegations about her character. You can emphasise the benefits of her relationship with the children and explain that this contact would continue even if the two of you split up because her rapport with the children is independent from your relationship as a couple.

The welfare officer and the court may want to know what the sleeping arrangements are, particularly if you live with a lover, or if she comes to stay regularly. What will be in the mind of the traditional probation officer is: are you influencing your children into being lesbian or gay. You need to think about how to play this. Many lesbians are not prepared to compromise themselves by denying their relationships. If you want to play discretion, then think about separate bedrooms for you and your lover. Or you may want to say your relationships are carried on outside the home. On the other hand you may want to present your relationship in a positive way, stressing your lover's involvement with the children, and the positive nature of her relationship with them. As one woman says 'I'll never regret leaving (the matrimonial home), nor my reasons for doing so, nor could I regret having had two children. I'm now building a new friendship and trust with them. They love my lover very much and miss her if she's not there.'

All children are affected to some extent by the close relationships that adults have, and even less prejudiced welfare officers may want to know how these are affecting the children. Some people think that all lesbians are into roles. They may believe, for example, that your lover is there as a substitute father figure. We suggest that you disillusion him/her as quickly as possible.

'Who would you choose, your children or your lover?' This is one of the most offensive questions that a lesbian mother can be asked. You may prefer not to answer such a question and get your barrister to object to it being put. However, if you do choose to answer it, the best way is to state that of course you put the children first in all situations, but the question does not arise since your children get many benefits from the relationship. You should also check whether the father is being asked if he would choose his new wife or cohabitee above the children.

Communal households and shared childcare

The courts do not look favourably on communal households whether they are lesbian or heterosexual. If you live in a communal household you should think carefully about how this is presented to the court and to the welfare officer. If you share childcare with other women you should present this in a positive way, stressing the benefits to the children, and how it is a sensible way to organise childcare if you work.

Stability

Where you are not in a regular relationship, then it maybe wise to stress that the relationships you have are kept separate from your child/ren's lives, and that you always prioritise your child/ren's interests. Although the courts do not like 'instability' as they call it, there is no reason for them to conclude that this will affect the child/ren. In fact a recent appeal was won by a lesbian mother, where it was suggested that she had 'unstable relationships'. The appeal judge concluded that there was no evidence that this affected the children. (*G v D* 1983)[4]

POLITICS

Lesbian mothers are often accused of trying to influence their children politically. This includes taking children on lesbian or women's liberation demonstrations, 'peace' demonstrations, anti-deportation demonstrations or anything that can be construed to be political. If you are alleged to be a separatist, you may be accused of using the case to fight your political battle, and of being a man hater. The best way to counter this is to produce a couple of men as witnesses, if possible. There is no reason why you should not take your children on demonstrations, providing that they are not coerced into going, or why you should not go yourself. In trying to limit this freedom the courts are undermining your civil rights, and your barrister should argue this.

CONDITIONS OF CUSTODY

You should also bear in mind that some lesbian mothers who have been awarded custody have had to agree to conditions which could infringe on their civil liberties. These include not taking children to demonstrations, not going to lesbian meetings, not living with a lover, or not having a lover to the house, or worst of all, having no contact with a lover at all. Another condition that can be imposed is a supervision order. This means that your childcaring will be watched over by a local authority social worker, who can visit you at home and see the children. You can refuse admission to the social worker, but this could go against you. S/he also has the power to apply to the court for a change in your custody arrangements.

Your barrister should object strongly to any conditions being put on your care and control. In one appeal case the court refused to make it a condition that the mother should not live with her lover, and this case should be quoted if necessary (*W v W* 1976).[5] Your barrister should also object to the imposition of a supervision order on you just because you are a lesbian. If necessary s/he should make it clear that you would be prepared to appeal against such an order. However, if you feel there is no alternative but to agree at this stage, remember you can go back to the court to get the order lifted.

AT COURT

Will your solicitor be at court?

You should ask your solicitor whether she will be going to court. She may be there for part of the hearing, but it is quite likely that she will not attend the hearing at all. If she doesn't there will be someone from her office who knows about your case – a trainee solicitor or a clerk. If at any time during the hearing you want to tell your barrister something, let your solicitor's representative know and she will pass the message to the barrister. You will probably want a note of the judgment, so make sure that your solicitor has someone there who can take the judgment down and give it to you afterwards.

Barristers

Your barrister and the father's barrister will probably do a lot of talking together on their own. This may make you feel that decisions are being made without your being consulted. This is standard procedure and there is nothing you can do about it. Your barrister should report back to you and consult you. If she doesn't ask her what has been going on. Be firm with her.

Bargaining

It is quite common for bargaining to go on right up until the time you go into court and there may be pressure on you to agree so that a court hearing is avoided. Any deals you are prepared to make must be discussed with your barrister *before* you go into court. This is the time when you are most vulnerable, because courts are very intimidating places when you are not used to them. It is good idea to take a friend with you.

Witnesses

Your barrister is not allowed to talk to your witnesses (except expert witnesses) and they are not allowed to sit in the court. They come in when they are asked to give their evidence and should then leave. Sometimes witnesses can stay in court once they have given evidence. You can ask the court if they can stay, although the other side can object.

In private

The court hearing will be in private ('in chambers') so only you and the father and your legal representatives will be there. This means that there won't be any publicity during the case. The only time when there could be publicity is if your case is an Appeal case.

The judge/magistrate can also ask questions at any time in the proceedings. Ask your barrister how you should address the judge/ magistrate.

Children

It is best if the children do not come to the court. It may be distressing for them, and the court will disapprove of them being there. However, make sure they are ready to come to court in case they are needed to see the judge.

Sue Beasley

AFTER THE HEARING

After the hearing there will be discussions and consultation about access arrangements. Whether you have lost or won your case you will be in no state of mind to think about the details, so have them already worked out in your mind. Think about what access visits you want if you do not have custody and what access arrangements you can cope with if you have custody. (See Chapter 6 for what you can do if you lose.)

OUTLINE OF PROCEDURE

Barrister for petitioner/appellant (you, if it is your application; see Glossary):

1. Outlines the facts of the case and directs the judge's attention to affidavits and reports.
2. Puts your case.
3. Questions you.
4. You are cross-examined by the father's barrister.
5. You are re-examined by your own barrister.

Your witnesses are then called, and:

1. Questioned by your barrister.
2. Cross-examined by the father's barrister.
3. Re-examined by your barrister.

Barrister for respondent (see Glossary):

1. Questions the father.
2. The father is cross-examined by your barrister.
3. The father is re-examined by his barrister.

The father's witnesses are called and are:

1. Questioned by the father's barrister.
2. Cross-examined by your barrister.
3. Re-examined by the father's barrister.

The father's barrister sums up his case.

Your barrister sums up your case.

The judge may retire to consider evidence.

The judge returns with his judgment.

THE RIGHTS OF CHILDREN IN CUSTODY CASES

The wishes of children in custody disputes is a difficult area because children can be manipulated and bribed. One lesbian mother said: 'One of the children, who was 10 at the time, decided that she would like to live with her father in America (he promised her a horse if she did) and she stayed there for a year . . . she didn't get the horse, so she came home.' Moreover, in a lesbian custody case the father can set children against their mother by instilling into them anti-lesbian prejudices.

When parents separate, children tend to have little say about who they will live with, as the court decides what is in the best interest of the child/ren. The court does not have to listen to the child/ren's wishes but the older the child/ren are the more likely the court will take their wishes into account. The age varies, but it is usually 9 or 10 upwards. One mother regained custody of her children in an Appeal case because they were so emphatic about wanting to live with her and not with their father, even though they were both quite young. When your child/ren say they want to live with you it may be a good idea to try and get their views put to the court. In order to avoid being accused of manipulating your child/ren you could arrange for them to speak to a third party, e.g. a social worker or court welfare officer, or to write a letter to the court. They could ask the court welfare officer to include their views in the welfare report. Judges (but not magistrates) may talk to child/ren in private giving the child/ren the opportunity to say who they would like to live with.

In divorce proceedings, if the court decides the case is particularly difficult or complicated it can order that your child/ren be separately represented. A Guardian ad Litem (see Glossary) will be appointed.

This may be a relative or a social worker or the Official Solicitor. That person must report to the court what in her opinion is best for your child/ren and if the child/ren disagree they should ask that the court be informed accordingly.

Child/ren can always seek independent advice from a solicitor on any decision made by parents or the court (see Resources list). Children cannot initiate court proceedings other than wardship. If your child/ren find themselves in the custody of their father but want to live with you, they could make themselves wards of court. In order to do this they would have to appoint someone to act as their 'next friend' because only an adult can sign wardship papers. The next friend could be a relative, social worker, teacher or lawyer. Being wards of court means that the court makes all the major decisions about your child/ren's life including who your child/ren should live with. Such an application should therefore be considered *very carefully*. If your child/ren are already wards of court and are unhappy living with their father or other relative they can approach the Official Solicitor who can apply to vary the order.

PAYING FOR LEGAL ADVICE AND REPRESENTATION FOR CHILD/REN

1. Applying for Green Form Advice and Assistance

If the child/ren are over 16 they can apply for Green Form Assistance on their own. If they are under 16 years the application should be signed by an adult, generally a parent.

2. Applying for Legal Aid

Normally child/ren will be represented by an adult (next friend or Guardian ad Litem) and this person will therefore make the application for Legal Aid.

WHOSE RESOURCES ARE ASSESSED? (Green Form Advice and Legal Aid)

For children over 16 only their own disposable capital and income is taken into account. For child/ren under 16 their resources are assessed together with the resources of any person who is responsible in law for maintaining them. However, their resources won't be taken into account if that person has a contrary interest to the child/ren.

THE OFFICIAL SOLICITOR

In a custody dispute (mainly where the child/ren have been made a ward of court) the court may decide to appoint the 'Official Solicitor', who is a civil servant and a lawyer, to represent the interests of the child/ren. In reality this means that a representative from the Official Solicitor's office will write a report about the welfare of the child/ren. The representative is a civil servant but is not a lawyer or a trained social worker/probation officer. S/he will see the child/ren both on their own and with their mother and their father. In making her/his report s/he can also (with the approval of the court) use expert psychiatric evidence. The Official Solicitor will see and approve the report and will be represented in court by a barrister. The representative who writes the report usually comes to court and your solicitor can insist that s/he does.

A lesbian mother who lost custody where the Official Solicitor was involved wrote about her experience:

'After my son Dean (who was then 12) was made a Ward of Court by his father (F), the Official Solicitor was appointed supposedly to represent his interests. Mr Jones, the representative of the Official Solicitor, spent a long time talking to Dean on his own, at his father's house where he had been staying when he was made a Ward of Court. He also spoke to me on my own, my lover on her own, and F and his lover together. I then insisted that he should visit Dean in my house as well in order that he could see how we got on together and how he was in his natural home environment. He would not have done this had I not insisted. I also thought that Dean was probably inhibited in what he said to Mr Jones because of his father being in the next room. Mr Jones obviously never considered these points, or had already made up his mind what was best for him anyway.

'My son and I were both taken in by Mr Jones's apparently friendly and understanding attitude, and in the end felt fooled and betrayed. Mr Jones acted like a friend and confidant to Dean, and told him that whatever the outcome of the case he could always talk to him afterwards if he was unhappy. When he did want to speak to him after the case, we were informed that he was no longer dealing with us and he would have to talk to a complete stranger instead.

'At the interim Hearing the judge had empowered Mr Jones to call in a psychiatrist if he thought it necessary. When I asked him if he intended to do so, he said no, because my son was "one of the sanest children he had ever met" which must be "largely due to the way you brought him up". I thought he was on my side but he still made his final judgment against me on the basis that Dean's father and his lover could provide "*at least the semblance* of a normal family". It seems that a "semblance of normality" is considered more important to a child than sanity!

'Despite the fact that recent studies show that the traditional family is no longer the 'norm', courts and Welfare Departments still cling to the idea that children should be brought up by a husband and wife with offspring living together under the same roof. Although F and his lover could not provide this ideal either, they were at least heterosexual.

'Mr Jones's sympathetic treatment did not work on my lover who is less easily taken in, so he became very cold and rude, like an interrogator. He asked her questions about our sex life and other insulting things. My lover felt totally pre-judged by him. His head was full of prejudiced stereotypes which he then proceeded to fit her into.

'As far as material comparisons went, Mr Jones described F's home as 'very comfortable' and mine as 'fairly comfortable'. He commented on the long walk from the station to my house – presumably it would have made a better impression if I had owned a car. There was no mention of the fact that F had not given me any form of maintenance for five years to help with Dean's material needs.

'Since the judge had been completely biased against me at the interim Hearing, my only chance of keeping my son was to have a Report from the Official Solicitor strongly in my favour. As this was not the case, it was obvious that I was going to lose him so I finally went back to court just to settle my access rights. Once again I felt unprepared and let down by Mr Jones because he did not appear in court himself, but had a barrister to represent him. The barrister was arrogant, hostile and homophobic from the start. Despite his final judgment, Mr Jones had at least realised the importance of the relationship between my son and me enough to recommend in the report that I should have good and frequent access. However his barrister completely ignored these recommendations. He stated that I was a "bad influence" on my son because I was encouraging him to come back to me, and pressed for minimal access. He did this without consultation and against the wishes of Dean who he was meant to be representing. F and his lover agreed to this despite the fact that I had always let them see him whenever, and for as long as, they wanted to. So, not only was my son taken away from me, but I was also denied reasonable access.

'In his report Mr Jones said that if my son did live with me there should be a supervision order put on me, but if he lived with his father it would not be necessary. Consequently there has been no follow-up to the court case despite the fact that Dean is still officially a Ward of Court. F and his lover have not acted on undertakings they agreed to in court regarding Dean's welfare, and he has not been contacted once by the Official Solicitor's representative to see how he is getting on or if he is happy.

'Finally, my advice to other lesbian mothers and co-parents/child carers is to be very wary of welfare officers and representatives of the Official Solicitor and not let themselves be taken in, as I was, by a sympathetic approach. Most welfare officers are heterosexual and will probably not share your attitudes; they are generally looking for a 'normal', heterosexual family setting for a child, or for the nearest approximation to it. So it is very important to stress the positive things you can provide for your child, and the negative aspects of the alternatives. However distraught you may be feeling remember that it is not your unhappiness that they are concerned with, but the *appearance* of a happy home.'

RESOURCES

Expert witnesses

Contact Rights of Women Lesbian Custody Group for suggestions.

Children's legal problems

The Children's Legal Centre deals specifically with children's legal problems.

The Children's Legal Centre
20 Compton Terrace
London N1
Tel: 01 359 6251

6
What You Can Do If You Lose

Most lesbian mothers who lose custody feel bitter for years afterwards. Don't let your distress prevent you from insisting on having the access that you want. It is best to work out what you would want in the event of losing before it happens. When deciding what access you want, bear in mind school holidays (even if the children are currently of pre-school age), festivals, e.g. New Year, your child's birthday, your birthday, Bank Holidays, and any important times you have celebrations. What ever you arrange, make sure you keep it regular. Try not to mess the child/ren around. You should insist on staying access at weekends. Usually you could expect to be granted access every other weekend, half the school holidays (including half terms) and alternate festivals. If you happen to live just round the corner you ought to be able to see the child/ren on some weekday evenings too.

After a contested case it will be difficult to cope with making arrangements for access with the father. If you anticipate that he will make things awkward, do get access defined by the court. Include the time you can collect the children and the time they are to be returned. It saves a lot of hassle and anxiety in the long run.

Intermittent parenting is not easy. Not knowing what size shoes your child/ren take, or whether they have had a tetanus jab recently can be upsetting and embarrassing. One woman told us,

'Unbeknown to me my daughter had started wearing a bra which she had left in my dirty-laundry bag. When I came across this "unknown" article of clothing in the laundrette I presumed that it had been left behind by someone else and had got mixed up in my washing, so I handed it in to the attendant. It was very embarrassing to have to go back the next week and say that it belonged to my daughter – especially as someone else had claimed it!'

Discipline may become a problem because you may not want to fall out with your child/ren in the short time you are together.

Relations between your child/ren and your lover will need your vigilance and possible intervention. Children can make adults' lives very uncomfortable if they choose. Whose side will you take in a dispute?

You may feel their education or their health is being neglected. They may be sent to you in poor clothing as a way of forcing you to buy them something to wear. The court welfare officer (if you had one) may be prepared to intervene on your behalf in any situations which are difficult to resolve between you and your ex-partner, e.g. disputes over access dates. If you are not happy with the access arrangements you can apply to the court to vary the access order (see below).

Your children may well express the wish to live with you/return to you. This is the most difficult thing of all to handle. It is unfair to raise false hopes and yet it is hard to stamp out such wishes. If you are convinced the children are unhappy then you could apply for a variation of the custody order (see below). Bear in mind the child/ren still have to live with their father, having made their wishes clear – not an easy situation.

Losing custody can be completely devastating. You may feel your life has been destroyed and you cannot cope any more. It is very important to get support at this time and to realise that things will get better. These are two quotes from women who lost custody:

'I'm from a working-class family with *no* financial resources. As soon as I left my matrimonial home, I hit with incredible clarity, the reality of having *no safety net.* Nowhere to run to. Since then I've had homelessness which added to the stress of "the custody battle" and I became very ill. I'm left with low physical stamina, but I'm a *dyke*, I'm all in one piece. I'm happy. I now have a cheap, lovely flat, a good relationship with my children, and I have my sanity.'

'When I lost custody of my child I felt completely destroyed. I lost my job and got evicted from my house. It was a very hard time, but I have survived and recovered. Although they could stop me living with my child, they could not stop the love between us, in fact it has grown stronger.'

APPEALS

No custody order is final. If a parent loses custody or is denied all access s/he may be able to appeal against the court's decision or apply for it to be changed. It is not easy to appeal and there are certain rules and guidelines governing the right of appeal. More often than not if you have received Legal Aid, the certificate will cover your solicitor/ barrister advising you on the merits of an appeal. An appeal usually involves your barrister making oral representations to the court on the law and/or facts relevant to your case and is rarely a rehearing of all the evidence.

1. Appeals against custody orders

From Magistrates' Court to Divisional Court or Family Division of High Court.

From High Court and County Court to Court of Appeal.

From Court of Appeal to House of Lords.

No permission ('leave') to appeal is required. Certain guidelines are set down in the case of *B v W* (1979) by the House of Lords for cases dealing with the custody of children. This judgment said that the appeal court ought to be particularly cautious of interfering with the discretion of the lower court and should only reverse or vary it if the court thinks the lower court's decision was 'plainly wrong'. In order to win the appeal you have to have good grounds. These grounds could be that the judge at the first hearing did not take all the evidence into account or disregarded the recommendations of the welfare report. If your appeal succeeds the court will either make the appropriate fresh order or send the case back to the lower court for them to make the order.

2. Appeals against access orders

Appeal is to the same court as for custody. It is generally difficult to appeal against an access order, because the judge/magistrate will have seen and heard all the parties give evidence and made a decision on that basis. First of all you must obtain leave to appeal unless you were refused *all* access at the first hearing. Leave to appeal against a reasonable and defined access order will only be granted in cases where it can plainly be shown that the judge/magistrate came to the wrong decision.

Time limits

Time limits for lodging appeals vary from four to six weeks from the date of the decision, depending on which Act proceedings have been brought under.

Appeals to the European Court of Human Rights

It might also be possible for lesbian mothers to consider taking a test case to the Court of Human Rights in Strasbourg. Britain is a signatory to the European Convention on Human Rights 1950 and the British courts could be in breach of the European Convention in depriving lesbian mothers of custody. Certain Articles in the Convention give rights of freedom of thought, expression and association with others plus the right to respect for family life. It could be argued that where the English courts impose conditions on lesbian mothers such as not to contact/live with their lovers they could be in breach of the Convention. Appeals to the Court of Human Rights must be made within six months.

Changing the order (variation order)

An application for changing a custody or access order can be made at any time by any party to the proceedings. Your lawyer will refer to this as varying the order. It is not an appeal but rather a further application to the same court which made the custody or access order. It is usually on the ground that there has been a change of circumstances since the original hearing. For example, a father might apply when a lesbian mother who got custody started living with her lover or if he found out after the hearing that she was a lesbian. A mother could also apply if the father was given custody and the child/ren were unhappy living with him. If you and the child/ren's father reached an agreement without a disputed hearing (this is known as a consent order) then this can also be changed if it proves unworkable.

'Not under the same roof'

Legal Aid

Legal Aid is available for appeal and variation applications but you will have to convince the Law Society that you have sufficient grounds of appeal to merit them extending your Legal Aid.

7
Money Matters

As we make clear throughout this book, lesbian mothers can be forced into agreements about their children that heterosexual mothers would not even have to consider. This also applies to sorting out money matters or dividing up jointly owned property.

For many of us, keeping our child/ren is the only important issue. Some men will try to use the threat of a custody dispute to get out of paying maintenance. Others will let you have the child/ren provided they can have the house! Trying to get what is yours may rock the boat and how far you are willing to argue about money may depend on how confident you are about keeping the child/ren. If you have been awarded custody of your child/ren or custody is not in dispute then you should think carefully about what financial assistance, if any, you want from the father. Do bear in mind however, that if you bring the case to court for maintenance then it could prompt the father into making an application about custody/access, which he might not otherwise have done.

You do not have to claim maintenance but bringing up children is an expensive business. Views on this vary. One woman who answered our survey said:

'My son's father did not pay me any maintenance for five years after we separated and I did not press him for it as I did not want to feel dependent on him, but at the same time I felt a lot of resentment towards him about it. This contributed to the breakdown of the relationship between us which ended in him going to court and getting custody. I think now that I should have insisted on maintenance in the beginning instead of just growing more and more resentful.'

However many women shared the experience of the woman who said, 'It wasn't until I started pressing the father for money that he went for custody'.

In this chapter we look first at maintenance (that is, regular payments of money) and then at the ways in which the law divides jointly owned property (e.g. a house, money in the bank, etc.). We also include information about making wills, covenants, and the social security benefits you might be able to claim.

MAINTENANCE

What you can claim

The law varies depending on whether you were married to your child's father. If you have been married then you could claim (a) maintenance for your child/ren; (b) maintenance for yourself.

If you were never married then you can only claim maintenance for your child/ren.

Most maintenance is paid on a weekly or monthly basis. If you are on Supplementary Benefit you need to consider whether it is worth claiming maintenance for you/your child/ren as it will be deducted from your benefit.

How you can claim it

Through the court
You don't have to have a Court Order for maintenance if you can come to an acceptable agreement but the advantages to you are:
1. If the man stops paying, then the court can enforce the Order (e.g. by ordering his employers to deduct the maintenance from his wages and to then hand it over to the court – this is called an 'attachment of earnings order').
2. The man can claim tax relief. This can be of indirect benefit to you because you can argue that he can therefore afford to pay you more.

A voluntary agreement
If you don't want a Court Order, but do want something in writing,

then enter into a written agreement. Your solicitor can advise you about this. Remember:
1. If the man does not pay, you will have to go to court.
2. The man cannot claim tax relief on voluntary payments (see above).

Maintenance for your child/ren

How much the father will be ordered to pay depends mainly on his income; your income (if any); and the child's age.

Your sexuality is irrelevant. It has nothing to do with maintenance for your child. The court should disregard any allegations made by the father about your lifestyle, but if you are living with your lover, and she contributes to household expenses, the man may say that your lover's income should be taken into account. If you are worried that you will be cross-examined in court about your sexuality then tell your lawyer to object to such questioning. (See In Court Strategies.)

If you have never been married to the father
If your child is a Ward of Court then the court can direct that the man contributes towards the child's maintenance.

If you are involved in custody or access disputes then the court has no power to order the father to pay maintenance but if he agrees to do so voluntarily then you can have his promise to pay put in the court order.

If there are no other proceedings about your child and you want maintenance from the father then you will have to apply for an affiliation order in your local Magistrates' Court. The disadvantage of doing this is that before the court can order the payment of any money it has to make what is called a 'declaration of paternity', that is, it has to say the man is your child's father. This could prompt him into making an application about custody/access and you should therefore think very carefully before taking affiliation proceedings, particularly if you have any doubts about the identity of the child's father.

If you have been married to the child's father
If you have been married to the child's father then there are a variety of ways of getting maintenance. You can get maintenance whether or

not you are going to get divorced or judicially separated. You can apply for maintenance at any time until your child leaves school or finishes further education.

Changing the Order

Unfortunately, maintenance orders cannot be linked to the cost of living, so they do not automatically increase from year to year. If you need more money because your child is getting older, or to keep up with rising prices, you will have to ask the court to change the order. Another ground for asking the court to change the order is if there is a change in the man's financial circumstances. If his income goes up you should ask for an increase in maintenance. If his income goes down, however (e.g. he loses his job) he too could ask the court to change the order by reducing the payments.

If you are going for a change in the order, then where the father agrees to this, you will not have to attend court and a 'consent order' will be drawn up by your solicitors. If the man does not agree to changing the order then you will have to attend court to argue your case. Legal Aid is available to vary maintenance orders.

Maintenance for yourself

You can only claim maintenance for yourself if you have been married to your child/ren's father. He could argue that because you are a lesbian you do not deserve any maintenance and this is an argument that the court may listen to. The law has changed on this and it is now more likely that your 'behaviour' will be taken into account. The best way round this is to go for as much maintenance for your child/ren as possible. If you do manage to get maintenance from the child/ren's father you should think about insuring it. You should ask the father to take out a life assurance policy which will provide a sum of money for you or your children on his death. *You* can also insure the maintenance payments in case he stops paying or reduces the amount because he loses his job or his income goes down.[1]

THE FAMILY HOME AND OTHER PROPERTY

Again, the law is different depending on whether or not you were married to the child's father. If you were married and are involved in divorce/separation proceedings then it is usual to sort out property matters at the same time (although there may be two separate court hearings). You do not have to be rich to have matrimonial property. For example, a council tenancy is treated by the law as property in the same way as a privately owned house.

Where you lived with your child/ren's father is called 'the matrimonial home'.

If there is an argument about who should keep the home, then the court's general approach is to let the parent with custody have the home so that the child/ren have a place to live. Often this is not possible (e.g. where the house is too expensive to run) so you should try to work out whether you can afford to stay in the house. If you cannot afford the house the court may make an order for sale and divide the money between you. The court can transfer the tenancy of rented accommodation to you. It can also transfer ownership of jointly owned property into your sole name. The court has wide powers, and a number of different orders can be made.

If you are involved in both custody and property disputes you may find that there is no procedure for the court to deal with both issues at the same time. You may have two court hearings – one about the children and one about the property. Going to court about property can be very expensive and so you should make sure that your solicitor advises you about the likely costs. You should do this even if you are on Legal Aid, as you may end up paying the costs of the case (see section on Legal Aid, pp. 37-8).

If you were never married to your child/ren's father but have lived with him in privately owned accommodation, whether you are entitled to any interest in the property will depend on whether you can show that the property is in both your names or that you made a direct financial contribution (for example you paid part of the mortgage). If you lived with the child/ren's father in rented accommodation and the tenancy is in his sole name then it cannot be transferred to you. If the tenancy was in joint names it cannot be transferred to you, but if he gives up his interest then a sole tenancy in your name can be created.

MAINTENANCE FROM YOU

If the father had care and control he has the same rights to apply for maintenance as set out above. You should make sure that you only pay what you can afford.

COVENANTS

A covenant has nothing to do with separation or divorce. It is a way of making payments to another person, usually a child, which has tax advantages. A covenant is a deed, i.e. a legally binding agreement, by which a person agrees to pay a sum of money to another person over a period of time. If certain rules are adhered to the person paying does not have to pay basic rate income tax on the money s/he is giving away. Therefore, if it is paid to a child it is tax free.

The main rules are:

1. The covenant must be for an indefinite period or for more than six years.
2. It must be for a fixed amount.
3. A parent cannot covenant money to any child under 18. Grandparents can make covenants to their grandchildren, and a friend or lover could make a covenant to your child/ren.

MAKING PROVISION FOR SICKNESS AND DEATH

Sickness

If you are incapable, the law automatically entrusts all decisions about you to your nearest blood relative, leaving your lover or friend powerless. You can give her control over your affairs by giving her a 'Power of Attorney' (you can get a form for this from a law stationers). You must give your lover or friend power of attorney when you are fully aware of what you are doing and it may continue to apply if you become mentally incapable.[2]

Who will look after my child if I die?

It is very important to make a will to ensure that your child/ren will be looked after by someone of your choosing and that any money or property you have goes into the right hands. If you do not make a will the child/ren's father (if you were married) or nearest relative e.g. grandparents will have a right to custody of your child/ren. However, if you make a will you can specify who will be the 'testamentary guardian' of your child/ren. When you die this person will act as joint guardian of your child/ren with their father if you were married. However, if the father or anyone else, say a grandparent, does not approve of the testamentary guardian they can apply to the court for custody. Even though someone else can apply for custody it is better to appoint a testamentary guardian because it is a clear statement of your views which a court would have to take into account in a dispute.

Financial provision for child/ren and lover

If you contribute financially towards the maintenance of a child and/or another woman, it is a good idea to take out a life assurance policy naming who is to benefit, so that when you die they will receive some money. If you are married and you die without having made a will any money and property you own may go to your husband. If you are divorced or have never been married it will go to your children. So if you want to make a provision for a lover/friend you should make a will.

If you have been contributing towards the maintenance of your lover or her child

If you have not made a will and you were contributing towards your lover and/or her child's maintenance they may have a claim over any money or property you leave. Likewise if your lover or friend dies without leaving a will you may have a claim over her money or property. You do not have to be a relative to claim but you do have to show 'financial dependence'. However, the legal fees could be substantial, so it is much better to leave a will.

...more mums are more fun......

Sue Beasley

How to make a will

You can get a will form from a stationer but if you do not follow the correct procedure the will will be invalid. You can get Green Form legal advice and assistance (see Legal Aid) to make a will, so if you are eligible you could get a solicitor to draw up the will for you. Make sure you keep it in a safe but obvious place. You can ask your bank or solicitor to keep your will for you, and you can keep a copy of it at home.

8
Adoption, Fostering, Guardianship and Becoming Pregnant

ADOPTION

When the court considers whether or not a person should adopt a child, the first consideration, as in custody cases, is the welfare of the child. In adoption cases you can assume that the court will have the same reaction as it does in lesbian custody cases i.e. it will be prejudiced against lesbians bringing up children.

Adoptions are arranged either by a local authority or a registered adoption agency. Most of them are as prejudiced as the rest of society. However a very few inner city boroughs have policies which enable lesbians to adopt/or foster child/ren. At the moment these are confined to the London boroughs of Hackney and Camden but social service departments in other areas may look at individual cases on their own merits. The Hackney policy states that 'prospective adopters and foster parents should be recruited on their merits as care-givers, irrespective of being lesbian'. It carries on to say that 'lesbian applicants should be assessed in terms of their capacity to provide warm/loving/caring conditions and not in accordance with an arbitrarily heterosexist view of what constitutes a "normal" upbringing'.

Many local authorities and adoption agencies will allow a woman on her own to adopt a child; children available for adoption by single people are usually either older children or children who are considered difficult to place. Stringent procedures of assessment take place before a local authority or adoption agency recommends that a person should be allowed to adopt a child. For example, your medical records will be checked, so if you decide to deny or hide your lesbianism you will have to be prepared for probing questions, and you should be sure that your lesbianism is not on your medical records. If you are going to long-term foster or adopt through your local authority you have to be approved by an adoption panel on which there will be lay members, social workers, elected councillors and a medical officer. If the local authority or adoption agency you have approached thinks that you are a suitable person to adopt a child the court will usually accept their recommendation.

The procedure for adoption

When you adopt a child you become that child's legal parent. One person alone or a married couple can adopt, but two single people cannot apply jointly to adopt a child. Many agencies first invite prospective adopters to individual or group sessions before allowing them to apply to adopt a child. Before you are allowed to adopt, s/he must live with you for at least three months. During this time you will both be monitored by the local authority or adoption agency.

Adoption is a legal process and the court has to make a formal adoption order. There has to be parental consent to an adoption order (although this can be waived in certain circumstances), but in most cases the parents will not know who the proposed adopter is, so they will not be able to object on the grounds of your lesbianism. All adoption applications are heard in private and all the information is confidential. A Guardian ad Litem (see Glossary) represents the child at the hearing to 'safeguard the interests of the child'.

Private placements

Not all adoptions have to be arranged by a local authority/adoption agency. A parent can place her/his child with a relative or friend and that person can then apply to adopt the child. The local authorty must be notified and will monitor the placement, so again, whether a lesbian will be approved by the local authority will depend on the local authority's attitude.

FOSTERING

You do not need the court's approval to foster a child. However whether you are considered suitable or not may depend on whether the local authority has a non-discriminatory policy, as with adoption. Again, where the local authority has no such policy it may consider you on an individual basis.

Fostering can, like adoption, be arranged privately. However you have· a duty to notify the local authority, so, again, whether you are considered suitable as a foster mother will depend on the local authority's attitude.

CUSTODIANSHIP

Since 1 December 1985 individuals have had the right to apply to. a court for legal custody of a child if the child has had her/his home with them for a certain period, or the person with legal custody of the child (usually the 'natural' parents) agrees they should have custody. The length of time for which the child must have had her/his home with you to qualify for this varies from three months to three years, depending on whether you are related to the child and whether the person with legal custody agrees. The only people who cannot apply for a custodianship order are the 'natural' parents of the child; this includes the father of a child whose parents aren't married. You can apply to the High Court, County Court or Magistrates' Court for a custodianship order and legal aid is available (see section on legal aid, see pp. 37-8). The court can make access orders in favour of the mother, father and/or grandparent of the child, and orders for maintenance of the child.

You might find custodianship useful in a number of situations, e.g.

1. If you've been sharing a home with your lover's or friend's child for some time and something happens to your lover or friend (e.g. long-term illness or death), you could apply for custodianship of the child.
2. If you've been sharing a home with a relative's child, e.g. your sister's or daughter's child.

The custodianship order would give you most of the parental rights over the child but would not be as final as an adoption order, i.e. it wouldn't break the legal link between 'natural' parents and child. Obviously, you could face difficulties in obtaining custodianship if your lesbianism were raised as an issue in the case.

If you are the natural mother of a child and someone else is given custodianship, you can ask for access. You can ask the court to end the custodianship order if there has been a change in circumstances.

BECOMING PREGNANT

There are two ways of finding sperm donors. One is through the medical establishment (Artificial Insemination by Donor) and the other is to find a donor yourself (self-insemination).

Self-insemination

Self-insemination is an easy, simple way to get pregnant, but it may be a problem finding donors. If you know the donor, you must consider whether he could ever claim custody of the child as the father. It is possible to use more than one donor so that you cannot easily identify the biological father. If the donor has an established relationship with the child you need to remember that he could claim custody as the father. A pamphlet and advice on self-insemination can be obtained from the self-insemination group at Women's Reproductive Rights Information Centre (see Resources).

Artificial insemination by donor (AID)

The advantage of AID is that the donor is totally anonymous, so there is no danger of a father being around to claim custody. If you are thinking about getting pregnant through AID you can get in touch with a number of organisations that do this for lesbians or single heterosexual women (see Resources).

RESOURCES

Self-Insemination

For a pamphlet on self-insemination contact:
  The Self-Insemination Group
  Women's Reproductive Rights Information Centre
  52/54 Featherstone St
  London EC1
  Tel: 01 251 6332

Artificial Insemination by Donor

An agency that does not discriminate against lesbians is The British
Pregnancy Advisory Service. The address of their head office is:
  BPAS Head Office
  Austy Manor
  Wootton Wawen
  Solihull
  West Midlands
  Tel: Henley-in-Arden 3225

Lyn May

The address of the London BPAS office is:

  2nd Floor
  58 Petty France
  Victoria
  London SW1H 9EU
  Tel: 01 222 0985

and they have branches throughout the country.

Another agency which provides AID for women with or without partners is:

  Pregnancy Advisory Service
  11–13 Charlotte Street
  London W1
  Tel: 01 637 8962

9
Nationality and Immigration

British nationality and immigration laws are racist, sexist and heterosexist. The law is very complicated and what follows is only a very rough outline. If in any doubt about your and/or your children's position, you should seek advice from a reliable source (see Resources for suggestions).

YOUR NATIONALITY

There are four categories of British nationality under the British Nationality Act 1981, but only one, British citizenship, gives you the 'right of abode'. Right of abode means you can enter the UK as of right and come and go freely. If very restricted circumstances apply, you may have the right of abode even though you aren't a British citizen. In most other cases you'll be subject to immigration laws which will control your entry to and settlement in the UK.

If you're an EEC national or Irish citizen you'll have greater freedom of movement and more rights than anyone except a British citizen. However, the UK government can in effect exercise immigration control over Irish people through the Prevention of Terrorism Act 1974 which contains wide powers to detain and exclude people from the UK.

WHAT IS IMMIGRATION CONTROL?

Immigration control means anything from a limit on the time you're allowed to stay in the UK to conditions on your stay, e.g. a prohibition on working. You can also be deported (sent out of) or removed from the UK in some circumstances, though there is a right to appeal against this. The powers of deportation and removal are used mainly against black people and people of colour.

CAN YOU AND/OR YOUR CHILDREN BE DEPORTED IF YOUR HUSBAND IS DEPORTED?

If your and your children's right to be in the UK depends on your husband's right, you could be in danger of deportation as members of his family if he is deported. If you're divorced from him and your children live with you, you and they can't be deported on this ground. You have a right of appeal against a decision to deport you, but there is no legal aid available. Some women have successfully fought deportation with the help of good legal representation (see Resources), their MP and the campaign work of friends and relatives, who have helped publicise their cases and have raised money to cover legal costs. The threat of deportation can put a lot of strain on you but you can get support (see Resources for suggestions).

HOW DOES SEPARATION AND/OR DIVORCE AFFECT YOUR RIGHT TO REMAIN IN THE UK?

Separation or divorce will only affect your right to remain if this depends on your husband's right to be in the UK. For example, if you came into the UK as the dependant of a man with limited leave to stay (e.g. student, work-permit holder, self-employed person) you won't be able to remain as his dependant once your limited leave runs out if you separate or divorce. However, you may qualify to stay in your own right. This puts you in a very difficult position if you're forced to leave the matrimonial home because of his violence, as the Home Office doesn't take your reason for leaving into account.

If you came to the UK after 26 August 1985 as the wife or 'fiancée' of a man settled here, you will have been given an initial limited leave of

12 months. If you leave him before you get indefinite leave to stay *and* have 'recourse to public funds' (Supplementary Benefit, Housing Benefit, housing under the Housing (Homeless Persons) Act), you may not get your limited leave to remain extended and may be in danger of deportation. So make sure you get advice from a reliable agency, *before* you claim benefit or ask the council to house you as a homeless person.

If you have an independent right to be here, separation/divorce won't affect your position. If in any doubt about your position, get advice from a reliable agency (see Resources).

IS IT WORTH APPLYING FOR BRITISH CITIZENSHIP?

You may have a right under immigration law to be in the UK even though you're not a British citizen. You may also have a right to become a British citizen if you wish and if you fulfil certain conditions. There are both advantages (it gives you more rights here) and disadvantages (it costs money and you could lose citizenship rights in your country of birth) in becoming a British citizen.

HOW CAN YOU BECOME A BRITISH CITIZEN?

You may be able to become one by *registration* or by *naturalisation*. They are different means to the same end and both cost money. You may have a *right* to register if you fulfil certain conditions. There is no right to naturalise, i.e. it's up to the Home Secretary whether or not to grant you citizenship and you have to meet certain conditions, e.g. you have to be of 'good character'. There's no definition of this so it depends entirely on the opinion of the Home Office, although they'll consider things like criminal convictions and your general financial position. Your lesbianism could be taken into account, if they know about it, though in 1981 a Home Office statement said that 'homosexual activities within the law' would not 'normally' be taken into account.

YOUR CHILD/REN'S NATIONALITY

Is your child a British citizen?

If your child was born or adopted in the UK *before* 1 January 1983, s/he is a British citizen. If s/he was born after that date, s/he may not be a British citizen.

You could find yourself in a situation where your children are British citizens, but you are not. If you are then ordered to be deported, you won't be able to stay in the UK on the basis of their citizenship. So far the Home Office hasn't allowed this as a compassionate ground for letting someone stay here. So British citizen children can end up being forced to leave the UK in order to stay with their mother.

What can you do if some of your children are living outside the UK?

If you're married to the children's father, your unmarried children under 18 may be allowed to join you in the UK and to settle here where you are 'settled' (i.e. have indefinite leave to remain). Otherwise they will be given leave to enter the UK for the same period as you. It's more difficult if you are divorced or separated from the child's father. In this case your child/ren will only be able to join you in the UK if you have had 'sole responsibility' for them.

How can your child become a British citizen?

S/he may have a *right* to register as a British citizen if certain conditions are fulfilled. Otherwise, s/he may still apply but s/he won't necessarily get it.

When should your child apply for British citizenship?

Preferably before s/he reaches 18, because after that s/he may lose the *right* to register and may only be able to apply for naturalisation, which has extra requirements.

G A Neslen

WHAT IF YOUR LOVER OR FRIEND HAS ENTERED THE UK FOR A TEMPORARY PERIOD OR IS LIVING OUTSIDE THE UK OR EEC?

She will not be allowed to remain in the UK beyond the temporary period or to enter the UK on the basis of her relationship with you. However, she may be able to stay or enter for a period in some other capacity, e.g. as student, work-permit holder, self-employed person, or if she marries a British citizen or man who is settled here. If the

Home Office suspects a 'marriage of convenience' it could question the validity of the marriage and, if successful, could deport her.

LEGAL ADVICE

It is very important to get reliable legal advice on your immigration position from an independent agency which is experienced in this area of law, e.g. your local law centre, Joint Council for the Welfare of Immigrants, or UK Immigrants' Advisory Service (see Resources for addresses and further details). They should be able to help you or recommend someone in your area who can advise you. A solicitor who does a lot of divorce or custody work may have very little experience in immigration and nationality law. You should check on this, as divorce could affect your and your children's right to stay in the UK.

There is no legal aid for immigration hearings and appeals, but you can get advice under the 'Green Form' scheme if you come within certain income/capital limits. You will be able to get free advice and representation from a law centre or the JCWI.

RESOURCES

Advice on nationality and immigration

For advice on nationality and immigration contact The Joint Council for the Welfare of Immigrants (JCWI) or the UK Immigrants' Advisory Service who will either give you advice or put you in touch with a law centre, advice agency or solicitor with experience in immigration/nationality work.

Joint Council for the Welfare of Immigrants
115 Old Street
London EC2
Tel: 01 251 8706

UK Immigrants' Advisory Service
7th Floor
Brettenham House
Savoy Street
London WC2
Tel: 01 240 5176/7/8/9

Deportation

For legal advice see above.
For general help and support contact:
Women Immigration and Nationality Group (WING)
c/o Joint Council for the Welfare of Immigrants
115 Old Street
London EC2

Books

See Further Reading and Information at end of book.

10
Police Powers

If the police know that a woman has children they often use it against her, for example by threatening to keep her at the police station overnight when there is no-one at home looking after the children. If they know you are a lesbian they can be particularly abusive. We have therefore included a chapter on police powers so that you know your legal rights, and know when these are being abused.

The Police and Criminal Evidence Act 1984 gives the police far wider powers of stop and search, detention and questioning as well as some new powers. These powers will make it even easier for the police to harass women who are black or of colour, Irish women and lesbians. Some of the powers the police have are:

- to stop and search you in the street or in a vehicle for stolen goods, for 'offensive weapons' (e.g. a knife), or 'prohibited articles' (e.g. a false credit card);
- to raid your home whether or not you are suspected of an offence, if they have a warrant, and while there to remove *any* 'evidence' of any crime;
- to arrest you on the spot if they suspect you of committing any offence however trivial AND if they believe you've given a false name and address, or if you do something which they decide is an 'affront to public decency', e.g. kissing another woman in the street.

If the police stop you but do not arrest you, you do not have to give them your name and address. However, there are many exceptions to this general rule.

AT THE POLICE STATION

You can be strip-searched by a woman police officer if the police believe you have something on you that you are not allowed to keep. This could be anything from an offensive weapon to combs, key-rings, etc.

The police can also authorise an 'intimate search' of the 'body orifices' – nose, mouth, vagina, anus – if they believe that you are concealing either certain types of drugs (e.g. LSD or heroin, but not cannabis) or an object which you might use to injure yourself or others. They are supposed to get a doctor or nurse to carry out such a search but if this isn't 'practicable' (when will it ever be?) it should be done by a woman police officer. The police can use 'reasonable force' while carrying out such a search.

The police can take your fingerprints, even if you have not been charged; they don't have to get your consent and can use 'reasonable force' to take the prints. They can take your photograph without your consent but they are not meant to use any force in doing so. You can be held for questioning for up to 96 hours (four days) without being charged if you are suspected of committing a 'serious arrestable offence' (24 hours in other cases). This can mean any arrestable offence (see Glossary) if it has resulted in, or could result in, death or serious injury or serious financial loss to someone, or is a 'threat' to national security or public order.

N.B. The police decide what a 'serious arrestable offence' is.

You are entitled to ask the police to advise someone of your choice of your whereabouts at their expense. You are entitled to see a solicitor, talk to her in private and have her present while you are being interviewed. *But* if you are being held for a 'serious arrestable offence' the police can deny you both these rights on various vague grounds for up to 36 hours. If you are being held under the Prevention of Terrorism Act 1974 you can be denied access to a solicitor for up to 48 hours. If the police do deny you either of these rights, keep asking for both and keep asking why they are being refused. Remember you do not have to answer any questions or say anything. If you remain silent it cannot be used against you later.

YOUR CHILD/REN

It is very unlikely that you will be able to see your child/ren while you are being held in a police station. If the police know you have a family, they are likely to threaten that the children will be taken into care if you don't 'admit everything'. This is to put pressure on you and to bully you into confessing to something. If the police don't know you have children, it may be a good idea to keep quiet about this so that they have one less hold over you. You could simply ask them to contact a friend or relative who will be able to arrange for your children to be collected from school, to be looked after, etc. You can of course do this even if they do know you have children. If the police refuse to contact the person you name, or if you don't know anyone who will be able to look after your child/ren temporarily, the police could apply for a Place of Safety Order which would ensure that your child/ren are taken to a 'place of safety' e.g. a children's home or foster care (see p. 16).

At the very worst, the police can deny you all contact with the outside world for 36 hours or 48 hours under the Prevention of Terrorism Act. Once this time is up, either you will be able to make arrangements for your children through a solicitor/friend, or you will be out of police custody. Given all this, you should try not to be bullied into admitting anything to the police. In the long run, it could prove worse for you if you admit things and are then charged with something serious for which you could go to prison.

IF YOU ARE SENT TO PRISON

If you are sent to prison either on remand or after receiving a prison sentence, this does not affect your custody rights. If you think you might go to prison, then make sure that there is someone who is willing to take care of your children. If there is no-one to look after them, then they may end up being taken into care. Once you are out of prison, you can apply to have the Care Order discharged. The fact that you go to prison, and are a lesbian, does not necessarily mean that you will lose custody of your children. A woman in this situation was recently awarded custody, even though the father had a reasonably 'normal' and respectable family situation for the child.

ASKING THE POLICE FOR HELP

The police are renowned for being extremely unhelpful if they are called out to deal with racial attacks or domestic violence. If you have any such problems with the police you can make a formal complaint about them. If you have been injured you can make an application for compensation to the Criminal Injuries Compensation Board. Ask a solicitor or Law Centre about these possibilities.

RESOURCES

Police

For advice and help on problems with the police contact
Lesbians and Policing Project (LESPOP)
38 Mount Pleasant
London WC1 0AP
Tel: 01 833 4996

Prison

For support for black women in prison contact
Black Female Prisoners Scheme
141 Stockwell Road
London SW9
Tel: 01 737 5520

A campaigning group for women in prison is
Women in Prison
c/o Unit 3
Cockpit Yard
Northington St
London WC1N 2NP

A service for women who are or have been in custody and who live, or want to live in the Greater London area. They offer practical help, advice, and information on a wide range of issues.

The Women Prisoners' Resource Centre
Room 1
Thorpe Close
Ladbroke Grove
London W10 5XL
Tel: 01 968 3121

PART TWO

11
A Historical Background to Custody Disputes

Prior to 1839, the father's rights over his *legitimate* children were seen as absolute and natural, and the courts had no jurisdiction to award custody at all. Up until 1857 women as well as children were seen as their husbands' property, and the married woman could not own property, had no standing in court, and had no legal rights over her children. As far as an unmarried woman with a child was concerned, her child was considered the child of 'no-one', until 1891 when the House of Lords recognised that the mother had a responsibility under the Poor Law to maintain her child (*Barnardo v McHugh* 1891). 'Part of the reasoning was that the obligation imposed on the mother by the Poor Law to maintain her child gave her a corresponding right to custody.'[1]

The unmarried father had no rights to the child, until the Legitimacy Act 1959 gave him the right to apply for custody or access. He can now apply for access or custody under the Guardianship of Minors Act 1971.

From the mid 19th century onwards there were a series of piecemeal reforms which allowed married women certain property rights, introduced civil divorce, gradually extended the grounds for divorce that women could use against their husbands, gave married women some legal status and introduced some major reforms in the area of custody.

In 1839 the Custody of Infants Act gave married women certain rights in terms of claiming custody of their children. The Court of Chancery was empowered to grant a mother custody until the child reached the age of seven, and access until she came of age (21). Even then however the mother's sexual behaviour was a crucial factor which affected her rights, and if she had committed adultery she had no claim at all.

In 1886, with the passing of the Guardianship of Infants Act the rights of the mother to her legitimate child/ren were increased. This gave the mother the right to claim custody of her child/ren up to the age of 21, irrespective of whether or not she had committed adultery. It also directed the court for the first time to have regard to the *welfare* of the child. Thus the welfare principle challenged paternal rights, without extending the mother's rights of custody.

In 1925 the Guardianship of Infants Act established the principle of the welfare of the child as the first and paramount consideration and equalized both parents' rights to custody if they came before a court. The Act stated that '[the court] shall regard the welfare of the minor as the first and paramount consideration and shall not take into consideration whether . . . the claim of the father is superior to that of the mother, or the claim of the mother is superior to that of the father'.[2]

In part this Act giving the mother equal rights to apply to the courts for custody can be seen as a response to pressure from the 19th century feminist movement, the Women's Franchise League, and later feminist groups who were campaigning for equal rights in custody and divorce. However the establishment of the welfare principle as the *overriding* consideration gave the patriarchal state, as represented by judges, the absolute discretion to decide what the best interests of the child should be. It also gave the state the opportunity to define the role of motherhood.

The 1925 Act only gave women 'equal' rights to claim custody if they applied to a court. It did not alter the old common law rule that in the case of legitimate children parental rights were still vested exclusively in the father. In practice this meant that unless a mother had been awarded custody by a court, she had to obtain the father's consent to any major decision concerning the child, e.g. an operation, or passport for the child.

This inequality was not altered until the 1973 Guardianship of Minors Act in which the mother's rights were clearly stated: 'In relation to the custody or upbringing of a minor . . . a mother shall have the same rights and authority as the law allows to a father and the rights and authority of mother and father shall be exercisable by either without the other.'

Since the 1925 Act, whilst the courts were not supposed to consider the wife's adulterous behaviour as a bar to custody, they continued to do so until the late 1960s.

In 1950 Judge Wallington, when awarding custody of a two year old girl to a father, said that 'It could never be in the interests of the child to be entrusted to the care of a woman who had committed adultery' (*Willoughby v Willoughby* 1951).[3] In 1962 Lord Denning stated: 'This [good mothering] in itself is not always enough, one must remember that to be a good mother involves not only looking after the children, but making and keeping a home for them with their father . . . insofar as she herself by her conduct broke up that home, she is not a good mother' (*Re L (Infant)* 1962).[4]

However, by 1969 the Appeal Courts were overruling the lower courts' decisions of punishing a mother for adultery by depriving her of her children and the lower courts were beginning to disregard a wife's adultery in considering care and control. In *Re F* (1969)[5] Judge Megarry ruled that in spite of a wife having been 'impetuous and selfish' in committing adultery and leaving her 'fair-minded husband' after only 18 months, she could have care and control of her three year old daughter. He said: 'as a general rule it is better for small children to be brought up by their mother'.

This principle has been reiterated several times. In *B v B* (1975)[6] it was held that 'unless there was some really good reason children of this age (under 6) should be with their mother. That was the social norm.' In *Re K* (1977)[7] where custody was awarded to the adulterous wife of a vicar, Sir John Pennycuik stated that a mother 'not as a matter of law but in the ordinary course of nature is the right person to have charge of young children'. In the same case Stamp LJ said the mother is 'the natural guardian, protector and comforter of the very young'.

In *J v J* (1979), where the custody of a 5½ year old boy was in dispute, Ormrod LJ stated: 'At the age of 5½ years one would assume that the little boy would be happier on the whole with his mother than away from her.'[8]

12
Lesbian Mothers v the Courts

In 1921 the House of Lords refused to make lesbianism illegal, because they thought that if it was made visible it might encourage other women to become lesbians.

This attitude was expressed in a speech made by the speaker of the House of Lords: 'You are going to tell the whole world that there is such an offence, to bring it to the notice of women who have never heard of it, never dreamt of it. I think it is a very great mischief.'[1]

Very few lesbian custody cases are heard about. This may be partly because some lesbian mothers may avoid using the courts as far as possible, or they may be advised by the legal profession that they stand no chance of getting custody through the courts.

However, there have been a number of Appeal cases where lesbianism has been raised as the main ground why the mother should not have custody, and they have largely gone unreported in the Law Reports and Journals. Further, there are virtually no discussions or articles which raise the fact that mothers lose custody of their children merely because they are lesbians in the legal literature.

Such a lack of reporting and discussion of lesbian custody issues is not without significance. It serves to keep lesbian mothers invisible. In a 1976 case in the High Court the judge believed it must be 'rare' for a child to grow up in a lesbian household, when it is estimated that one in five adult lesbians may be mothers.

Further, it means the prejudice of the judiciary and legal profession towards lesbian mothers does not have to be confronted. As long as the issue can be kept hidden such judicial and legal prejudice remains unexposed and unchanged.

What follows is an outline and discussion of mainly Appeal cases

108

since 1976, that we were able to find through an extensive search. All except one of the seven Appeal cases are unreported. There may have been other unreported Appeal cases that we did not find, so this outline cannot be viewed as totally comprehensive.

PREVIOUS CASES

In 1976 a contested custody case was briefly reported in the Family Law Journal.[2] A mother living with her lover in a lesbian relationship had sought custody of her five-year-old boy. The mother had been separated from her husband for two years at the time of the hearing and the child had lived with her and her lover since the separation. After a hearing lasting six days the mother lost custody.

If the same criteria had been used as in heterosexual cases, no doubt the mother would have got custody. Both sides had an equally comfortable standard of living, and the child had been living with the mother for two years, so she had status quo. He was also of an age where the courts would usually consider he should be with his mother. The judge acknowledged the quality of the mother's care and concern for the child. However, lesbianism became the key issue as to why the mother should not have custody, and was the basis of the father's case. Three psychiatrists were called to testify to the effects of lesbianism on the child, two appearing for the father. The psychiatrist for the mother testified to the quality of the mother's and her partner's relationship with the child, and the trauma which would be caused by removing him from his established home, which he considered would be greater than any damage caused by a lesbian relationship. Also any possible teasing would be better coped with if he stayed with his mother.

It was also established by the mother's psychiatrist that the child had contact with heterosexual and male relatives with whom he could identify. On the father's side, however, both psychiatrists said that the child 'would have considerable difficulty growing up unblemished by his abnormal situation'. In delivering his decision the judge preferred to accept the opinions of the two psychiatrists who said that the child would be 'blemished'. Both of these psychiatrists showed considerable bias in the the presentation of their evidence, according to the law report, and made statements which have no foundation in fact. For example, it was suggested by one psychiatrist that the mother's lover was immature because of her closeness to her own extended family. It was also suggested that the child's psychosexual development would be put at risk by his mother and her lover sleeping in the same bed.[3]

The judge spoke of the gravity of damage from possible lesbian influence being 'inestimable' and said that the child might grow up to be 'ashamed and embarrassed by his mother'. He also spoke of the child learning to accept his mother, whilst not approving of her: 'It would mean the decay of society if people adopted the latter attitude. We definitely cannot have the approval. It would be detrimental, anyone might be influenced if it were approved of.'[3] He stated that the boy should live in a house which he could describe as 'normal' to his friends and that he would be less likely to be teased if he had a normal background. Further, if he lived with his father, no one need ever know of his mother's lesbianism. He talked of the boy needing to 'develop along *strong normal masculine lines*', and of 'difficult and uncharted waters'. He assumed that it is 'rare' for a child to grow up in a lesbian household and therefore, because of the unusualness of the case, it was necessary to rely on 'expert opinion'. The 'experts' in the case, as in later cases, did not however agree, and the judge chose the opinions that accorded most closely with his own views on the matter, rather than considering the reliability or otherwise of the evidence offered.

In the Appeal of *W v W* (1976)[4] the mother won her case for custody of her two daughters (twins) aged 11 at the time of the appeal hearing.

The basis of the father's case had been the mother's 'attachment to the Women's Liberation Movement, and her lesbian activities'.

In awarding custody to the mother the Appeal judges were careful to state that: 'the case turned on practical day to day grounds . . . and I hope no one will regard this judgment as containing any pronouncement for or against homosexual activities' (Ormrod LJ.) Sir John Pennycuick went even further when he stated that whilst he was not expressing any moral view on lesbianism or the Women's Liberation Movement he would not have hesitated to take the girls away from their mother 'if any acceptable or practical alternative had been available'. In particular it would seem that the judge did not want to appear to be giving a judgment in favour of a lesbian mother.

The case was decided 'on the narrow grounds of bricks and mortar and nothing else' i.e. the father's proposals for the accommodation for the children were found to be 'wholly unsatisfactory and unsuitable' (Ormrod LJ).

Further in an examination of the judgment and circumstances of the case considerable moral and social disapproval was expressed towards lesbianism.

The mother had been living with her two younger daughters and an older one (whose custody was not in question) since the father had left the matrimonial home in 1975 to live with his new wife. He had already divorced her some years earlier on the grounds of unreasonable behaviour, i.e. her lesbian and Women's Liberation activities and having extreme feminist literature in the house.

Earlier in 1976 the mother had lost custody in a lower court and the father had also got an order to exclude her from the matrimonial home. However, whilst waiting for her appeal to be heard, a temporary order had been made, allowing her to stay in the home, and to keep care and control of the children, on the condition that her lover had no contact with the children and did not come to the house.

The mother had lost custody on the assumption that 'her philosophy and way of life is such, that it is likely in the long term to bring them (the children) great unhappiness'. A number of highly biassed and prejudiced statements were made about the mother and her lover by the lower court judge. For example she was criticised for being 'obsessively wrapped up in herself and the feminist cause', whilst the father was applauded by the judge for holding 'strong and decided views'. Both the mother and her lover were described as being 'dangerous' or a 'dangerous influence', on the children, without any justification being offered by the court. The welfare report had made no recommendation but concern was expressed about the mother's 'anti-men' feelings.

In the main Appeal Court judgment, Lord Justice Ormrod stated that whilst they were considering the case 'with as open minds as it is possible to have on this type of issue' the mother ought to agree that, 'it is quite obvious that their lives are highly abnormal', and that it is 'simple common sense to say that the children ought to have a more normal life in a more normal family, amongst less vehemently minded people. It would be difficult to dispute that proposition.'

He reiterated that if the father could have made suitable accommodation proposals for the two girls then he would have got care and control.

He did however decline to put any conditions on the mother's care and control, as regards keeping the children away from her lesbian friends, since such conditions would be counter-productive as they would turn the mother into a 'martyr'. Perhaps more importantly, however, he felt that such conditions would under the circumstances be unenforceable, and the only way to enforce such conditions would be to remove the children from the mother altogether. It was hoped that the mother would use her 'good sense' to make sure her personal life did not affect the children too much.

Thus while the mother was given custody, because there was no alternative, the heterosexist assumption was still made that her views and lifestyle must be bad for the children.

S v S (1978)[5] was an appeal brought by a lesbian mother against a father who had won custody. The judge in the lower court had also preferred to rely on the 'expert' evidence of the father's psychiatrist who had never even seen the parties or the children.

This psychiatrist had stated that the children 'would be caused social embarrassment and hurt, and that it could be very harmful to them if it became known that there was a lesbian relationship between their mother and Ms D'. The children, aged 7½ (a girl) and 6 (a boy), had both clearly expressed their wish, via the welfare officer, to stay with their mother. The welfare report had recommended that the children stay with their mother, with a supervision order to the court welfare services which should be carried out by a man! Both psychiatrists had said there was no risk of the children being led into 'deviant' sexual ways if the mother was given custody, and the welfare report stated that the mother was capable of caring for the material needs of the children, whereas the father would have 'difficulty in this respect'. The father had admitted to indulging in 'abnormal sexual practices', but these were not put under scrutiny by the court, as the wife's lesbianism was.

This time the judge, in choosing to ignore the recommendation of

The fact that your husband has some abnormal sexual practices & that he has been violent towards you is not the issue ... your lesbianism is .....

Lyn May

the welfare report, and accepting the evidence of the father's psychiatrist, Dr Klassnick, gave as the reason for his judgment the social 'danger' to the children of being brought up by a lesbian mother, and referred to the case of *Re D (an infant)* (1977).[6] *Re D* was a case where a homosexual father refused to give permission for his ex-wife and her new husband to adopt his son. The case bears absolutely no relevance to lesbian mothers (Lesbianism has never been illegal, as has male homosexuality) bringing up children except that the man was a homosexual, and therefore considered a 'deviant'. The case went to the House of Lords. Lord Wilberforce, when giving his judgment, waiving the need for the consent of the father, said:

'Whatever new attitudes Parliament or public opinion might have chosen to take with regard to the behaviour of consenting adults over 21, these should not entitle the courts to relax in any degree the vigilance and severity with which they should regard the risk to children at critical ages, being exposed or introduced to a way of life which might lead to severance from normal society, to psychological

> stresses and unhappiness, and possibly even to physical experiences which might scar them for life.'

The judge in *S v S* referred to 'the dangers of children being exposed or introduced to ways of life of this kind, and to the possibility that such exposure might scar them permanently'. This statement goes far beyond the expert opinion offered in the case.

The appeal was brought on the grounds that the judge in the lower court had disregarded the recommendation of the welfare report, and had disregarded the evidence of the mother's psychiatrist who had actually seen the parties. Both judges who heard the appeal case, but particularly Lord Justice Orr, thought it was fair that the judge disregarded the welfare report recommendation, and that he 'preferred' the evidence of the father's psychiastrist, Dr Klassnick, even though he had not seen the parties involved, since the judgment was essentially 'a matter for the learned judge' to decide after hearing all the evidence.

The only complication in this case was that the mother originally denied her lesbianism (not suprising in the face of such prejudice) and only admitted it when the father produced a tape-recording of a telephone conversation she had had with him.

The mother, after initially leaving the matrimonial home because of her lesbian relationship, had returned to it to care for the children until custody should be determined by the court. She again, therefore, had status quo. In addition the judges chose to disregard her parental abilities, the provision of a good home, the wishes of her children the unsuitability of the father both in terms of the accommodation offered and his own sexual behaviour, and the recommendation of the welfare report, to make what can only be described as a moral judgment against lesbianism by rejecting the appeal.

The appeal case of *W v W* (1980),[7] however, produces slightly more liberal pronouncements on the part of the judiciary towards lesbianism. The appeal was brought by the father for custody of his son, aged three-and-a-half. The mother had been awarded custody in a lower court. Lord Justice Brandon stated:

> 'I do not think that this case ought to be decided on the basis that it

would be *harmful* to the boy to live with his mother, in a home where she is engaged in a lesbian relationship, although I do not think one can wholly disregard the fact that it is a somewhat unusual home.'

The father won his appeal on the grounds that he had had status quo of the child for most of his life.

Whilst lesbianism therefore was not raised by the judges as the deciding factor, one wonders whether the mother would have got custody if she had been heterosexual, given the young age of the child. It was also mentioned that the father had some interest in homosexual relationships, but the judge chose to disregard this because 'there is no evidence that this has any impact on his home life or the child's life'. There is no mention in the judgment of the welfare report recommendations.

E v E (1980)[8] was an appeal brought by a mother for custody of a boy aged six. The mother lost her appeal. Both parents had always worked and the child was called 'granny-reared', because he was looked after by his grandmother when his mother was at work. After they had separated, the child was looked after by 'other than either parent', but the judgment does not state by whom, so neither parent had a status quo situation at the time the case was first heard. The mother had been ordered out of the matrimonial home by her husband because of her lesbian relationship (a feature which commonly occurs in cases in our survey), and the divorce was brought on the grounds of her lesbianism. There were two welfare reports both recommending that the mother should have custody. The first was based largely on 'the shortcomings of the father's character, and the stronger character and discipline of the mother'. The second report still recommended custody to the mother, whilst drawing the court's attention to certain 'highly undesirable signs that the child exhibited', as reported by the father. These undesirable signs consisted according to the father of comments made about 'women kissing' and a preoccupation with 'the female anatomy'. Discussion with the mother suggested that the child was making such comments before she and her husband had separated. The Appeal judge Dame Elizabeth Lane was shocked at the mother's response, and stated that she could have understood it if the mother had responded to the welfare officer with 'good gracious me, this must be something the father had invented', or 'the little boy has heard something he should not have heard at school'. She stated that 'rather precociously the child is manifesting a curiosity about something which he cannot possibly understand, but which he may even at his age feel instinctively to be something strange or unusual'. It is in our view extraordinary that a judge could assume that at the age of six children are not interested in sexual behaviour. The judge was projecting her own views onto a child whose feelings on the strangeness and unusualness of the matter had not been ascertained.

The father was unsuitable on two counts: the shortcomings in his character, and the fact that he could not provide suitable childcare. The trial judge however had chosen to award him custody despite his unsuitability on the grounds that: 'he is obviously a young man (28) and no doubt capable of development, I have to consider the possibility that faced with these responsibilities he might rise to the occasion; the circumstances might bring out in him the necessary qualities . . . he might try and remedy his defects'. What his defects were, we are not told. The first decision and subsequent appeal were decided on the child's 'undesirable' interest in an 'unnatural relationship' and the speculative future effect on him of this relationship.

Dame Elizabeth Lane qualified her own homophobia by being careful to state that 'there is no rule or principle that a lesbian mother or homosexual father cannot be granted custody of a child. Indeed, I myself sitting at first instance, have committed the custody of children to such parents more than once.' Yet there was no apparent other reason for not giving the mother custody. Speculation was made as to the future effect of lesbianism on the child, and she referred to the comment of the first judge on possible future teasing of the boy: 'It would not be long before this little boy found himself to be the subject of taunts, and his anxieties would be aroused by the difference between his background and the others.' She concluded by a vague reference to risks: 'My inclination is to decide the case not on the personalities but rather that the child is getting on well where it is and not to expose it to the *risks* of putting it with the mother.' There is no reference to what these risks were. However, earlier she had stated that 'the way of life would not be right or natural', and that if he lived with the mother, 'he would learn more and more and it would fill him with dismay and would be very worrying and upsetting for him'.

Re P (a minor) (1982)[9] was an appeal brought by the father. The mother had been awarded custody of her six-year-old daughter in a lower court. The father could not actually have custody of the child (it is not stated why), but he wanted her to go into *care*, rather than remain with her mother. There were also allegations about the father's treatment of the child which 'were of such a character as to disqualify the father from having care of the child, if they were true'. We are not told what they were, and the bias of the courts in protecting the father's reputation, as in the previous case, is once again apparent. Since the father could not have custody the whole ground of the appeal was based on his objection to the child being brought up in a lesbian household.

The first judge stated: 'The only question that I have to ask myself is whether the *proclivities* of the mother and the lady with whom she lives are such as to make it undesirable in V's interests that she should be brought up in that home.' The judge then stated that before a child could be committed to care, it must be 'impracticable' or 'undesirable' that the child should be placed with an individual. Since it was not impracticable that the child should be with its mother, it had to be shown that it was undesirable. The first judge stated that since he had no evidence of the effect on children of being brought up in homosexual households he must use his common sense! The father's case was based on 'corruption' and 'reputation'. Dealing with corruption, the Appeal Court then went on to say that there was no statistical evidence to give any clue as to the likelihood of corruption, corruption being defined as 'that by force of example, or by erosion of that *instinctive* rejection of *devious* conduct, which upon the father's analysis inevitably resides in the normal mind, in one way or another the child is likely to come to harm'. The mother was described as 'sensitive and discreet' and 'not one of those homosexuals who as many do nowadays, flaunt their homosexuality'. Corruption was therefore dismissed as a reason. 'Reputation' was, however, considered differently, as Sir John Arnold, the Appeal judge, stated:

'One does not have to be a psychiatrist to appreciate that a lesbian household would quite likely be the subject of embarrassing conduct and comment, particularly among the child's friends. It may be, and I am prepared to assume, that it *is* a disadvantage of so *substantial* a character, that it can fairly be classed as a feature of undesirability so as to let in . . . the power of the court to make a care order.'

However, since the 'undesirability' of the alternative had also to be weighed, it was considered that the 'warm mother's care' was preferable to the care of a local authority, and that the mother should retain custody.

The other Appeal judge in the case, Lord Justice Watkins, went even further:

'This is neither the time nor the place to moralise or philosophise about sexual deviance and its consequences on those who practice it, but the possible effect on a young child living in proximity to that practice is of crucial importance to that child and to the *public interest*. I accept that it is not right to say that a child should, in no circumstances, live with a mother who is carrying on a lesbian relationship with a woman who is also living with her, but I venture to suggest that it can only be countenanced by the court when it is driven to the conclusion that there is in the interests of the child, no other acceptable form of custody.'

So this lesbian mother was able to retain custody basically by default (i.e. there was no alternative). The father was totally unsuitable, and for whatever reason could not have the child. The mother could provide a secure environment and warm loving care. At least this was acknowledged. There is no reference to a welfare report. A supervision order was however made by the Appeal Court, which is unusual, and it was stated that the future progress of the child must be carefully and discreetly watched.

Another unusual factor in this appeal was that reference was made to an Australian case. Lord Justice Watkins suggested that conditions might need to be introduced into the order as in the Australian case of *Campbell v Campbell* (1974) (see Chapter 16 on Australian cases) where the mother was ordered not to sleep overnight with her lover, or 'engage in acts of a sexual nature in the presence of the children, or anyone else who might report those acts to the children'. In *Campbell v Campbell* it was also ordered that the children be seen annually by a psychiatrist.

In the final and most recent appeal case, *G v D* (1983),[10] the appeal was again brought by the father against a mother having custody of her two daughters, who were six and seven at the time of the hearing in 1980. The mother retained custody. The case was widely reported in the press with almost total sympathy for the father. At the very first hearing the father was awarded custody, even though the children had been living with their mother all their lives, including the three years since she had been separated from her husband. The father had applied for custody of the children on his re-marriage, on the grounds that he could provide a more stable and *normal* home for them. This view was supported by the welfare report.

The first judge had believed that 'the long-term interests of the children would be better served by being brought up in an *ordinary* household with a father and mother (or mother-substitute) rather than in a household which consisted of two women living together in the way that the mother and (Ms C) were'. In 1982 a *variation* order was made and the mother got custody. There was a new welfare report, which recommended that the children live with their mother since they did not want to live with their father and his new wife, and access periods had been particularly difficult.

In the appeal case it was stated that: 'The children do not want to live with their father and their stepmother. That being so, the Court has to give very careful consideration indeed to whether it is wise, particularly in such an abnormal situation as this, to force the children into a way of life that they did not like.' The judge was careful to say however that this did not mean that cases ought to be decided on the views of young children; it was more to do with how they were reacting to the situation.

Lord Justice Ormrod stated:

'The mere fact of this homosexual way of life on the part of the mother is not, in itself, a reason for refusing to give her the control of her children, although of course it is a factor that one has to take into account and think about very hard. Experience shows, just as in this case took place, that homosexual relationships do tend to be even more unstable than heterosexual relationships are, in these days, and the result is that there is a good deal of moving to and fro . . . but there is no evidence whatever that the children have suffered at all as a result. Mr and Mrs G had two other children very much older, also girls (their custody was not in question) and I think there is not much evidence that they have suffered or been caused to suffer stress by the mother's association with other women.'

This is perhaps the most positive and *least* discriminatory statement yet made by an Appeal Court judge regarding lesbianism. Yet the whole judgment relies heavily on the 'children's wishes' being expressed *strongly*. Reference is also made to the persistent fight of the mother to get her children back which is described as very 'determined and manipulative'. We are left wondering whether, if the children hadn't expressed their wishes so strongly, and if the mother hadn't fought so hard, she would have got custody. Nevertheless it is the only appeal case we know of in which a lesbian mother can be said to have succeeded, despite her lesbianism, and despite there being an alternative.

SUMMARY OF REPORTED AND APPEAL CASES

The guiding principle in English custody disputes is the welfare of the child as the first and paramount consideration. Bearing this in mind a number of disturbing features emerge from the cases outlined previously.

First, lesbianism has been focused on as the dominating reason why the mother should not have custody, rather than an examination of the quality and care of the parental relationships. Further, a number of unfounded and speculative assumptions have been made about lesbianism, without these having to be proved. On occasion, the judges admit to being ill-informed, but then proceed to decide the case just the same on their own prejudices. In the first case discussed (1976) the judge referred to 'uncharted waters', and in the case of *Re P* (1982) the trial judge stated that in the face of lack of evidence he must use such 'common sense' as he possessed. In both these and other cases, however, lesbianism is attributed with a negative moral value, as can be seen from the language in which it is described.

In *Re P*, for example, the judge said: 'The only question that I have to ask myself is whether the *proclivities* of the mother and the lady with whom she lives are such as to make it undesirable that in the [child's interests] she should be brought up in that home.'

In *E v E* (1980), despite Judge Dame Elizabeth Lane saying there was no rule or principle that a lesbian mother should not have custody, she assumed that lesbianism would be 'instinctively strange and unusual' to a child, and that the lesbian way of life was 'not right or natural'. Further, in a number of cases lesbianism is described as 'deviant' (*S v S* 1978), 'devious' (*Re P* 1982), 'abnormal' (*G v D* 1983), and 'unnatural' (*E v E* 1980). Unfounded speculations are made about possible future effects on children in highly emotive and moralistic language. In the first case (1976) it was stated that the children might be 'blemished', in *S v S* (1978) that they might be 'scarred permanently', and again in the same case, that the children would be 'subject to social embarrassment and hurt'. In *E v E* (1980) it was said that the child would be subject to 'taunts' and in the 1976 case that the child might be 'ashamed and embarrassed' by his mother. In the US such speculations would be said to constitute an 'irrebuttable presumption' contravening the due process clause of the 14th Amendment to the Constitution, i.e. that they would prejudice a 'fair hearing'. Even in this country such assumptions could be said to contravene the rules of natural justice.

In a number of cases the judges make openly moral statements about their views on lesbianism, which suggest that, rather than considering the best interests of the child, they are more concerned with controlling the moral behaviour of society. For example, in *Re P* (1982) LJ Watkins stated: 'this is neither the time nor the place to moralise or philosophise about sexual deviance and its consequences on those who practice it'. He then went on to do just that when he said: 'but the possible effect on a young child living in proximity to that practice is of crucial importance to that child, and the *public interest*'.

In the 1976 case the judge stated: 'It would mean the decay of society if people adopted the latter attitude (i.e. approval of lesbianism).

Anyone might be influenced if it were approved of.' Again, in the US such moral assertions would be considered an invasion of the fundamental right to privacy (see chapter on American cases), and there have been several appeal cases in the States where the judge has not been able to deprive a mother of custody merely because her lifestyle does not accord with the 'average'.

Another disturbing feature of these cases is the use of psychiatric or psychological opinion to reinforce the view that lesbianism is a form of 'psychological sickness' or faulty personality development. Chief Judge Elizabeth Evatt of the Family Court of Australia, in her review of judgments on Australian lesbian custody cases (1980) stated:

'It is interesting to note that the most frequently called expert was the psychiatrist. This demonstrates yet another frequently held myth about homosexuals – that homosexuality is some kind of mental disease.' She further stated that: 'the usefulness of the expert evidence presented in some cases is doubtful. Two completely opposing views from experts of comparable experience are often presented' and 'the widely conflicting views presented in evidence seem to reflect the current state of feeling within the community, and allow the judge to choose and rely upon a view close to his own view of the matter.'[11]

This can be seen to have happened in both the 1976 case and *S v S* (1978) where, with conflicting expert evidence, both judges chose the views which accorded most closely with their own.

Further evidence of judicial prejudice towards lesbian mothers in the cases discussed above is the disregard for general principles that apply in heterosexual cases. In two County Court cases and one Appeal Court case the judgment disregarded the status quo principle in transferring the children from their mothers to their fathers. In three cases the children were under five (i.e. of an age when it would normally be considered that they should be with their mother) and in two cases they were six or under. In one case the wishes of the children were totally ignored (*S v S*). The recommendations of the welfare reports were also ignored in two cases, although this also happens in heterosexual cases.[12]

A further interesting, but not surprising, feature of these cases is that the father's behaviour and lifestyle were rarely put under the same scrutiny as the mother's. Indeed, in *E v E* (1980), despite the fact that the father was obviously thought to be unsuitable, it was speculated that he 'might' develop the appropriate qualities needed to bring up the child. Such positive speculation about the future behaviour of the father can only serve to emphasise how prejudiced the judiciary is in failing to give the benefit of the doubt to the lesbian mother. In nearly all cases (with the possible exception of child abuse), it is assumed it is better for the children to be with their fathers, whatever their behaviour or lifestyle. Where the father can provide a new wife or cohabitee and the *appearance* of a 'normal' or 'ordinary' family background, even if the new mother 'substitute' is a comparative stranger, this is considered even more preferable. A child may be removed from its familiar environment and close and loving relationship with its mother for this reason alone.

In the case of *G v D*, at the first hearing, it was stated that 'the long term interests of the children would be better served by being brought up in an *ordinary* household with a father and mother (or mother-substitute) rather than in a household which consisted of two women living together in the way that the mother and [her partner] were'.

In the 1976 case it was stated that despite the 'quality of the mother's care' the boy should live in a house which he could describe as 'normal' to his friends; and in *E v E* that the child should not be exposed to the 'risks' of living with his mother. In *Re P* the child was only given to the mother, because in LJ Watkins's view there was 'no other acceptable form of custody'. In this case, the mother's 'warm, loving care' was considered preferable to putting the child in local authority care, but a supervision order was made and it was stated that the child must be carefully watched. Only in *G v D* was it stated that the children's wishes were taken into account and the judge questioned whether it was wise 'to force the children into a way of life that they do not like' (i.e. living with the father and new stepmother).

From this review we can conclude that lesbian mothers only get custody by default, i.e. when the father is considered totally unsuitable by the court, or has no suitable accommodation for the children, *W v W* (1976), or when the children absolutely refuse to live with their father (as in the case of *G v D* (1983)). Looking at the cases from 1976 to 1983, there has been a slight shift in attitude in some of the judgments. In the most recent judgment, for example, there is no reference to children being 'blemished' or 'scarred for life', and in *Re P* (1982) the corruption argument is dismissed as a reason, since there is no statistical evidence to support this view. Indeed, if corruption refers to sexual abuse or paedophilia, far from there being any evidence to suggest that lesbians abuse children, there is plenty of evidence to suggest that sexual abuse is carried out by heterosexual males.

In a study done by the American Humane Association it was found that 90 per cent of all child sexual assaults were on girls, 22 per cent of whom were abused by men within their immediate household. A further 11 per cent were abused by male relatives living outside the household. It was also found that in 97 per cent of cases, the abusers were heterosexual men.

This classic study which looked at a sample of 1,100 cases of child sexual abuse, estimated that between 1 in twenty and 1 in 10 girls within the heterosexual family experience some form of father/daughter abuse (incest).

In the experience of the London Rape Crisis Centre, incest is 'a crime committed by heterosexual males with normal personalities who come from all races and classes'.[14]

Judges, court welfare offices, psychiatrists and social workers might do well to consider the fact that it may not be safe for children to grow up in the heterosexual family, when considering custody issues, rather than assuming that lesbians are a danger to children, and that the heterosexual family must be a better alternative.

13
The Myths

NATURAL AND UNNATURAL

Ideas about what is natural and unnatural in terms of sexual behaviour have changed over the years, across cultures and in different societies. And perhaps most importantly, they tend to be determined by the most powerful groups within a particular society.

Lesbians exist and have existed across different cultures, races and classes and the acceptability or suppression of lesbianism has varied historically and within different societies. In this country, from the historical evidence and the literature of different periods, it would appear that up until the 16th century lesbianism was tolerated to some degree. It was, however, viewed as inferior to heterosexuality. The Christian church, for example, did not regard it as such a terrible 'sin' as male homosexuality. The 'sin' for women was to wear male attire and step out of the acceptable female role. By the 19th century, female sexuality in general was regarded as virtually non-existent, so lesbianism was viewed by some sectors of society at least as an impossibility.[1]

It was only at the end of the 19th century, with the emergence of the natural sciences and theories of evolution, that some forms of sexuality came to be defined as 'unnatural'. The only purpose of sex for *women* became defined as reproductive, and anything else was classed as unnatural since it did not further the survival of the species. Male sexologists suggested that lesbians were really men born into women's bodies; a forerunner to a more recent 'explanation' that lesbians have something wrong with their chromosomes or hormones. They also produced the idea of the 'butch' or 'femme' lesbian. The butch, they

125

suggested, was really a man inside a woman's body, the femme being a very feminine type of woman, but with small hips unsuitable for childbearing.[2]

Later, Freud tried to explain lesbianism in terms of faulty personality development and early childhood experience within the family. Lesbianism became viewed less as a physical deformity and more as a psychological sickness. The 'unnaturalness', 'abnormality' and 'mental disease' theories are still prevalent today, and are still endorsed by certain sectors of society, as we have seen in the chapter on lesbian mothers v the courts.

In the early 1950s, one of the few large-scale studies was done on female sexuality. Kinsey (1953)[3] found that, far from lesbianism being 'rare', out of 5,940 American women studied, one quarter had had erotic responses to other women by the age of 30. Also, between 11 per cent and 20 per cent of unmarried women and 8 per cent and 10 percent of married women had had incidental or deliberate lesbian contacts between the ages of twenty and thirty-five. In general, the Kinsey study showed that approximately 10 per cent of the population is lesbian or gay.

Kinsey also disputed the earlier ideas of what was natural or unnatural based on observations of mammal behaviour:

'The impression that infra-[sub]human mammals more or less confine themselves to heterosexual activities is a distortion of the fact that appears to have originated in a man-made philosophy rather than specific observation of mammalian behaviour. Biologists and psychologists who have accepted the doctrine that the only natural function of sex is reproductive have simply ignored the sexual activity which is not reproductive.'

In 1976, the Hite Report, another American study done on female sexuality, produced findings similar to those of Kinsey. Hite's sample was, however, self-selected (i.e. women volunteered to fill out a questionnaire). Hite found that 8 per cent of her sample of 3,000 women between the ages of 14 and 78 preferred sexual relationships exclusively with women, and another 9 per cent defined themselves as bi-sexual.[4]

FAULTY PERSONALITY DEVELOPMENT

The 'faulty personality development' theory is still used against lesbian mothers and their lovers in court to try and discredit their fitness to bring up children. Earlier, and in cases in our survey, it has been suggested that the mother's lover was immature. The Freudian view holds that lesbianism is an immature form of sexuality, since the lesbian is fixated in the 'phallic' stage of development. She has not transferred her sexual desire onto the male.

Psychoanalytic explanations for this are, to say the least, confused, and totally unsubstantiated by any factual evidence. One 'explanation' offered is that the lesbian is 'fixated' on her 'dominating' mother, another that she has 'over-identified' with her 'dominating and distant' father, and has refused the feminine role.[5] In general, psychoanalytic theory totally fails to explain why the same families 'produce' heterosexual and lesbian children, and why 'classical homosexual-producing' families have children that become heterosexual.

From the false belief that lesbianism is just a form of immaturity or just an adolescent phase also comes the belief that all lesbians are neurotic and have inadequate personalities.

In 1973 the American Psychiatric Association eliminated homosexuality from its list of mental disorders, yet the myth that lesbians are at least neurotic persists. Contrary to such prejudiced theories, many studies comparing lesbians with heterosexual women have found that lesbians are more self-confident, less neurotic, more independent and self-sufficient than their heterosexual counterparts. These studies used a number of different standardised personality tests to assess women from both groups.[6] Dr DJ West stated in 1977 that: 'Masculine conceit, and the reluctance of male researchers to put their assumptions to the test, must be partly responsible for the conventional wisdom that asserts that love between women is neurotic, immature, unsatisfying, impermanent or destructively possessive.'[7]

CORRUPTION

Another belief is that lesbians 'by force of example' (*Re P*) or by direct sexual threat corrupt children. It has already been stated that all the evidence shows that it is mainly heterosexual men (97 per cent) who sexually abuse children. One researcher (Richardson 1981)[8], in looking at attitudes towards lesbian mothers stated that 'there are virtually no cases of female paedophilia homosexual or otherwise reported in the (relevant) literature'. Yet the belief still persists, particularly in the courts. In a case reported in the *Guardian* (16 January 1978), where a lesbian mother had access to her daughter, her lover was ordered to go to the other end of the house every time the girl went to the lavatory.

Allied with the belief of corruption by example is the belief that lesbians are 'promiscuous', hence the conditions often laid down by the court that the mother must not have sex in front of the children, or have her lover staying while the children are there. Why it should be assumed that lesbians have sex in front of the children any more than heterosexuals, merely underlines the prejudiced beliefs about lesbian sexual behaviour. Women are supposed to be passive and dependent on relationships with men. In contrast with this traditional and acceptable role for women, lesbian sexuality and relationships are independent of men. Hence lesbians are assumed either to be pseudo-men and to take on aspects of male sexual behaviour, or the sexual aspect of the lesbian identity becomes totally exaggerated. Thus lesbians are viewed as primarily sexual beings and nothing else. As has been seen in the cases discussed in Chapter 12 on Lesbian Mothers v the Courts and our survey, the courts are voyeuristically obsessed with what the lesbian mother does in bed, and whether the children know about it.

INSTABILITY

Allied to the myth of the promiscuous lesbian is the belief that lesbian relationships are more unstable than heterosexual relationships, as was suggested in the case of *G v D* (1983). Some of these beliefs about lesbianism are transferred directly from stereotypical beliefs about male homosexuality. Such stereotypical beliefs include promiscuity, unstable relationships, an interest in predatory and anonymous sex (e.g. cottaging) and the confusion of male homosexuality with paedophilia. Whatever the basis of these beliefs as far as male homosexuality is concerned, there is no reason for transferring these qualities to lesbians.

In order to counteract the prevalence of such myths, a number of studies have been done on lesbian sexuality since the early 1970s. For example, FE Kenyon (1970)[9] found that lesbians do not differ from heterosexual women in patterns of monogamy and non-monogamy, and that they value emotional satisfaction above other possibilities, in common with heterosexual women. Other studies found similar patterns and showed that *being female* is what influences lesbian sexual behaviour and relationships. Therefore lesbians have little in common with male homosexuals (see M Freedman (1971) and S Schafer (1977).[10]

MOTHERING

Other studies have looked at mothering patterns in lesbians and compared them with mothering patterns in heterosexual women. Being a lesbian has often been viewed as in direct contradiction to the role of motherhood. This is an extension of the beliefs that lesbians are primarily sexual beings and nothing else, and also that lesbians as pseudo-men are incapable of mothering. Goodman (1973)[11], in comparing lesbian and single heterosexual mothers, states that 'the similarities of motherhood for both lesbian and non-lesbian mothers far exceed the differences and where differences do occur it would seem they are linked to social roles, discrimination and oppression with regard to lesbianism, rather than to differences in sexual preference'. Other researchers have come up with similar findings. For example, E Lewin (1979)[12], comparing 43 lesbians and 37 single heterosexual mothers, found a significant similarity in ways mothers met the challenge of daily life, and in their perceptions of their situations as single mothers'. In a later study (1981), which again looked at mothering patterns, she found that one of the few differences between lesbian mothers and single heterosexual mothers was that lesbian mothers are subject to increased *stress* through fear of loss of custody.

Again, RL Rees (1979)[13], in comparing 12 lesbian and 12 single heterosexual mothers and their children between the ages of 10 and 20, found no significant difference in parenting style.

PSYCHOSEXUAL DEVELOPMENT, OR HOW TO INFLUENCE YOUR CHILDREN WITHOUT REALLY TRYING

What psychologists call psychosexual development may be defined as:
1. Gender identity, that is, people's concept of themselves as male or female.
2. Sex-typed behaviour, that is, those behavioural features which are supposed (in the minds of some psychologists anyway) to distinguish the sexes.
3. Sexual object choice or orientation, that is whether a person becomes lesbian, gay or heterosexual (Rutter 1980).[14]

Some schools of psychological thought put great emphasis on early childhood experience as the determining factor in later psychosexual development and identity. In particular these theories emphasise the immediate family environment and parental figures as having the greatest influence on a child's future identity. Lesbian mothers may be accused of having a negative effect on a child's psychosexual development, or putting the child's psychosexual development at risk, as in 'A Case of Heads He Wins – Tails She Loses'.[15]

SEXUAL ORIENTATION

One of the greatest fears that underly the courts' decisions is that lesbians will influence their children 'by force of example', or by the 'absence of a father figure', to grow up lesbian or homosexual. This is also related to the corruption argument discussed earlier, and could again be an explanation of the conditions that lesbians should not have sex in front of the children, as the courts fear children might imitate that behaviour.

Some social learning theory stresses the importance of role models of young children in determining later sexual orientation. In the eyes of the courts, the lesbian household is providing inappropriate models of sexual relationships for the child. In addition, psychoanalytic theory states that boys need a father to be jealous of by the age of five (otherwise 'sexual inversion', i.e. homosexuality, might occur). Girls need a father-figure in order to transfer their sexual desires away from the mother onto a male-figure. Leaving aside the question of whether it is desirable that children should grow up to be heterosexual (no doubt the courts think that it is), neither of these theories have been borne out by statistical research, and they remain totally unproved. Yet they continue to be used in 'expert evidence' against the lesbian mother.

In a number of recent studies that have looked at indications of future sexual orientation in children of lesbian mothers compared with children of single heterosexual mothers, no difference was found between the two groups. In a recent British study which compared 37 children from lesbian households with 36 children from single heterosexual households (Golombok *et al.* 1983)[16], it was stated that:

'The findings of the study have been consistent in showing no difference between children reared in lesbian households and children brought up by a single heterosexual parent, with respect to gender identity, sex role behaviour or sexual orientation. The lack of difference seems to negate the hypothesis that children brought up by an actively lesbian mother are likely to show psychosexual anomalies.'

Similar research findings have been done in the United States by Martha Kirkpatrick (1981)[17] and B Hoeffer (1981)[18], both of whom looked specifically at sexual orientation and found no significant difference between the two groups.

The findings of these studies are not surprising, given that many lesbians and gay men see their sexual identity as a positive choice they have made as adults. Many of them have come from heterosexual families themselves. The view that sexual orientation is determined by early childhood experience and/or parental models is now questioned by many psychologists in the face of much opposing evidence. They would also question that children can be seen as passive receivers who automatically take on the role models provided by their parents. It is now recognised that there are many other influences on children and they select and make choices according to a variety of factors.

GENDER IDENTITY

Similar arguments outlined above have been used against lesbian mothers in terms of their children's gender identity (whether the child sees itself as a boy or girl). Freudian theory states that unless a boy has a father-figure around the age of five (the start of the oedipal phase), his gender identity may be seriously affected. It was suggested in one case in our survey by a court welfare officer that two little boys would grow up to be transvestites in their twenties in the absence of a father-figure. In 'A Case of Heads He Wins – Tails She Loses' (1976) it was suggested that only with his father could the boy 'develop along strong normal masculine lines'.[19] The same arguments could also be directed at single heterosexual mothers, particularly in the case of boys. Early role model theories also say that boys need a father-figure with whom they can identify. Many studies done on father-absent families do not, however, bear out this hypothesis. Also, studies done on children who have been incorrectly sexed at birth (Money 1965 and Hampson 1965)[20] show that gender identity is already fixed by the age of one-and-a-half and is virtually impossible to dislodge after the age of two. It has been suggested that boys in particular do not get their gender identity from their fathers (who, even in the nuclear heterosexual family, aren't around for most of the time anyway), but from general social influences outside the home, and in the different treatment of boys and girls from birth onwards.

GENDER-TYPED BEHAVIOUR

Numerous psychological tests have been devised to assess 'appropriate' gender-typed behaviour for girls and boys, examining such factors as the clothes children wear, the toys they play with, and the friendships they make. Assessments are often made on highly stereotypical notions of what toys for example, girls and boys should be playing with, e.g. dolls and Wendy houses for girls, cars, football, action men and guns for boys. In the studies quoted above, however, there was no significant difference found in the gender-typed behaviour of the two groups. On the positive side, in the British study (1983),[21] it was found that children of lesbians were less stereotyped in terms of their gender roles. Whilst they all played with toys appropriate for their sex, they also played with more 'sex-neutral' toys.

SOCIAL STIGMA

In the review of cases it was suggested that the Appeal Courts, at any rate, tend to focus on the effect of social stigma on the child, as one of the main reasons why lesbian mothers should not have custody of their children.

The argument is couched in many different forms e.g. that the child's relationship with her/his peers might suffer (*E v E* 1980), that children would experience social hurt and embarrssment in the neighbourhood (*S v S* 1978), that they would be the subject of embarrassing comments and taunts (*Re P* 1982 and *W v W* 1976); also that it is preferable for children to be *seen* as growing up in a 'normal' home where they can bring their friends.

Whilst this report would not deny that there is anti-lesbian prejudice from some sections of the community, this is no justification for the judiciary to support such prejudice. D Richardson (1981)[22] states in her examination of attitudes towards lesbian mothers:

'We might in any case want to question the emphasis placed on the stigma which children of lesbian mothers might face, particularly when it is used as a justification for the removal of the child from such a home environment. Children are stigmatised for all sorts of reasons, if they are mentally or physically handicapped, illegitimate, from an ethnic minority group, being too fat, too thin, too small, too tall, if they speak with a different accent and so on.'

The fact that they are stigmatised in this way does not, however, mean that they are removed from their mothers. There is also the assumption made by the courts that children will *always* be the subject of teasing, if it is known that their mothers are lesbians, and that where it does occur they will not be able to cope with it. Green (1978)[23] in a study on 21 children of lesbian mothers and transsexuals found that few children were teased because their mothers were lesbians (three) and where they were, these were only isolated incidents they could cope with adequately. For example, a child who was told that his mother was a lesbian replied 'So what', and there the matter ended. The British study also looked at peer group relationships and children's relationships with other adults outside the households, and found these similar to those of children in single heterosexual households.

In some US judgments, far from the social stigma argument being used as an excuse to remove children from their mothers, it was felt that children would be better able to cope with any hostility from the community if they stayed with their mothers (*Belmont v Belmont* 1980). Underlying the social stigma argument is the assumption that the heterosexual environment must be better for children to grow up in, and that there are no positive effects for children growing up in a 'nonconventional' household. One positive effect found in the British survey, for example, was that the children of lesbians tended to be more tolerant of others' differences, e.g. in terms of race, sexual orientation, etc. It is probably questionable, however, whether the courts would view this as positive.

HOW THE PRESS MAINTAINS THE MYTHS

The press coverage of lesbian mothers and custody cases seems to be a mixture of sensationalism, incredulity (lesbians can be mothers? shock-horror), and anti-lesbian hostility. For example, an article in *The Times* reporting that research has shown that children brought up by lesbians aren't any different from children brought up by heterosexuals is given the title 'Growing up "safe" with lesbians'. The use of quotation marks around the word safe implies that whatever the research shows, they don't believe a word of it.

One custody case where a lesbian mother was awarded custody of her daughters was widely reported in the papers. The *Daily Express, Mail,* and *Mirror* all picked up the same theme: 'A father wept yesterday after hearing two judges . . .' and ended with 'the girls' mother left court with her lesbian friend, "I'm over the moon," she said'. So even though the judges and welfare officers had stated quite clearly during the hearing that in their opinion the girls would have a more stable life with their mother, the papers clearly directed the readers' sympathy to the poor grieving father. The father was portrayed as an ordinary Mr Nice Guy who had suffered the dual trauma of his wife leaving him for a woman and his daughters being brought up by a woman whom the papers described as 'a Militant Feminist' and 'an ardent Women's Libber'. The papers then went on to report at great length about the father's and his new wife's ('I'm just a Marks and Spencer sort of woman') ordinariness, and their suitability as parents despite what the judges and welfare officers had said in court and the overriding factor that the two girls wanted to live with their mother.

The *Sunday Express* wrote a virulently anti-lesbian article about this case entitled 'No child should suffer this trauma', coming out with all the old chestnuts about children being 'corrupted' by being around lesbians, and how they will be outcasts in a predominantly heterosexual society, taunted by their friends at school etc. The way the article starts is interesting: 'Court battles over the custody of children are always distressing and often damaging to everyone involved but how would you feel if your ex-husband or wife chose to set up home with someone of the same sex and then won custody of the children?' A similar sentiment appears in an article about the organisation 'Families Need Fathers' in the *Guardian*, which implies that if a woman becomes a lesbian it's somehow the ultimate insult for the man who suffers dreadful traumas, becomes suicidally depressed and more prone to accidents, so therefore the lesbian mother should be punished by not being allowed to be anywhere near her children.

There is a real double standard in the reporting of custody cases. In an article in the *Sun* entitled 'Gay Mum can keep daughter aged 5, girl gets warm care says Judge' the mother is praised as 'a private sort of woman' who 'did not flaunt her homosexuality' but in another custody

Lyn May

case where a father wanted restrictions put on the children's access visits to their mother so that her lover could not be present, most of the papers made much of the fact that the children called their mother's lover 'Auntie . . .' and didn't know that they were lesbians. So a lesbian mother must not be open about her lesbianism but on the other hand there is something suspicious if she keeps it quiet too.

Luckily, considering the way the press report most lesbian custody cases, the majority aren't reported at all. Lesbian mothers losing custody cases don't seem to be considered newsworthy. We couldn't find any articles about the majority of lesbian mothers who lose custody of their children and the suffering they go through as a result.

The only publication to have articles where lesbian mothers were portrayed as ordinary, everyday sort of women (one even appeared to be wearing a Marks and Spencers jumper in a photo) were *Outwrite* and *Spare Rib*, both papers written and edited by women. Both these publications have let lesbian mothers speak for themselves about their relationships with their children, problems with custody and access, in a way the national press presumably finds too boring or unsensational to bother with.

14
The Survey

As lesbian-feminist mothers and legal workers living and working in the lesbian community, our own knowledge and experience has informed both the area of research and the questions asked. We wanted to delve deeper into what we already know to be a problem; to describe the experiences of women in this situation; to show the bias of the legal and welfare institutions in our society; and to use the information we obtained to campaign for change.

DESIGN OF THE SURVEY

It was decided to conduct the survey through a fairly lengthy and detailed postal questionnaire. While it might have been preferable to have conducted face to face structured interviews neither the time nor the money available to the project allowed for this. It was also felt that a postal questionnaire would guarantee complete anonymity, and that some women whilst being prepared to write down what had happened to them might not be prepared to talk about it to a stranger.

Inevitably, there are drawbacks to a postal questionnaire, ranging from the average return rate, which is only 30 per cent, to a misinterpretation or misunderstanding of the questions. Having to fill in a lengthy questionnaire may be intimidating to many, if not the majority of the population! It was necessary to rely on women's motivation to tell of their experiences. Many were willing to do so (and some even stated that it was a relief to put it all down on paper), others were no doubt put off either by the length, or because they felt the questions did not apply to their situation, or the areas covered by the questions proved too personal or painful to answer. Also, whilst all steps were taken to assure women of confidentiality and anonymity, there were still some who were worried about putting anything down in writing.

The questionnaire consisted of 15 areas with 5 to 17 questions in each. Many questions required simple yes or no answers, or ticks in boxes, while others were more open-ended questions in which the respondents were asked to describe their situation, or express their views.

A detailed instruction sheet was supplied with the questionnaire, particularly to explain legal terms. Despite this, there was still some misinterpretation or confusion, e.g. some women were confused about which court had heard their case (which is not surprising given the complexity and mystification of the English legal system). An initial questionnaire was designed and pretested on a very small sample (five) but because of concern about finding a large enough sample anyway, the pretesting had to be kept very small. One of our main problems was to try to reflect the wide range of circumstances and experience within custody disputes, as well as to obtain detailed and in-depth information that might be useful for lesbian mothers fighting custody battles in the future.

Inevitably some of the answers raised many more questions that needed to be asked, but this survey can only be seen as the beginning of research into all the issues surrounding lesbian custody.

AREAS OF INVESTIGATION

It is well-known to lesbian mothers at least that there is bias in the legal and welfare systems. The aim of the survey was to find out how that bias operates.

1. The legal profession

The outcome of what happens in a lesbian custody dispute may to a certain extent depend on how women are advised by solicitors and barristers and how their case is fought; we were therefore interested to know how women were advised or received by the legal profession (if they were approached) and whether this had affected their case.

2. *Welfare reports*

If cases did get as far as the courts, we were interested to know whether there was a welfare report, and how this might have affected the mother's case. We also wanted to know how welfare officers viewed lesbians and lesbian relationships, and whether this affected their report. In addition we were interested in the mother's assessment of the welfare officer's knowledge of children and how much time they spent assessing the mother-child relationship and the children themselves.

3. *Psychiatric reports*

We were interested in whether there had been any psychiatric reports, what their approach had been, and what effect they had if any.

4. *At court*

We looked at what happened in court, and what factors were focused on in the dispute.

5. *The father's situation*

We asked detailed questions about the father's situation and behaviour. We covered the areas of childcare, his own behaviour on the break-up of the partnership, including violence, sexual behaviour, paying maintenance and so on. We wanted to know whether these were also considered factors in the case.

6. *Outcome on custody, care and control*

We were interested to know what the outcome of the dispute was both in and out of the court; what reasons had been given by the court, or if agreement was reached out of court, what had been the factors affecting that agreement.

7. *Access*

We were also interested in access arrangements, whether these had been ordered by the court, or reached through agreement between the parties, and what problems there had been if any.

8. *Social services, schools, housing, police and other agencies*

We asked lesbian mothers whether they had any problems with other social and state institutions, and how these had affected them.

9. *General information*

We wanted to know what women's experience had been of being involved in a custody battle, or if they had come to an agreement, or got custody by not admitting their lesbianism, how this had affected them. We also asked if they felt their case had been affected by class, race or their financial situation. We asked about their living situation at the time of the dispute, to find out if this had had any effect on the outcome. In addition we asked about ages and sex of children. Although we unfortunately omitted to ask the year in which the dispute took place, many women gave that information and this emerged as an important indication as to whether the attitudes of the courts or other agencies had changed.

FINDING THE SAMPLE

Given that many lesbian mothers, or lesbians caring for children always live with the fear, at the worst, of having their children removed, or, at the least, of being put under surveillance by the welfare authorities, it is not easy to find a sample willing to fill out such a questionnaire. London Lesbian Line receives several hundred phone calls a year from lesbians who feel unable to leave their marriages, and who have to remain absolutely secret about the fact that they are lesbians for fear of what would happen to their children. Action for Lesbian Parents (a national group) also receives many requests for help. Both Lesbian Line and this organization receive phone calls from women who, in order to protect their relationship with their children, may never act on their desire to love women. In addition, the attempts to ensure the absolute invisibility and/or denigration of lesbianism by our social institutions and popular media made it difficult to publicise the survey. Only one women's magazine responded to our request to publicise the survey. All the others failed even to reply to our initial letter. Publicity was therefore largely confined to the gay, lesbian and feminist press, both in London and nationwide, which has limited distribution networks. Adverts were sent to all the lesbian and gay organisations that we knew existed (thanks to London Lesbian Line for this) and questionnaires were sent to the lesbian mothers' groups that already exist, or are forming in London. One hundred questionnaires were distributed and 36 were returned within the time limit specified. Given the painful and sensitive subject matter of the questionnaire and its length, this was considered a good return.

We have no way of knowing how many mothers have actually been through a legal custody dispute. Many lesbian custody disputes never get as far as being fought out in court, and those that do are rarely reported. Nor do we have any idea of numbers where lesbianism might be a factor in care or place of safety orders. This organization receives several phone calls a week, as well as letters, requesting information and referral to solicitors over custody or care disputes where lesbianism could be an issue. In addition, many women remain in the closet (secret about their lesbian relationship) during and after custody proceedings, so that it has never been raised as an issue. The estimated size of the lesbian population is between one in five and one in ten (Kinsey, 1953).[1] Out of these one in five may be mothers.[2]

ANALYSIS OF FINDINGS

Information was obtained from 36 questionnaires. Some details of specific cases have been omitted in order to protect the women and children involved. All the disputes in this survey took place between 1976 and 1984 except for one which took place in 1971.

Numbers involved

Our analysis was based on the experience of 36 lesbian mothers, and involved 64 children.

Disputes over custody, access or care

Out of these 36 mothers, 32 had been involved in a disagreement over custody, access or local authority care at some point. Twenty-nine of these were about who should have custody of the children. Two involved local authority care orders, and one was a dispute over the father's access to the child.

TABLE 1
Type of disputes

Disputes over custody and access	29
Disputes over access only	1
Disputes over local authority care	2
No dispute over custody or access	4
Total numbers	36

Disputes over custody

All the 29 cases of disputes over custody involved, or could have involved the issue of lesbianism, in the sense that the father knew the mother was a lesbian, and was prepared to use it in the dispute to get what he wanted. All these disputes involved a custody disagreement with the father. In one case a third party (the mother-in-law) threatened to intervene, but later withdrew.

Who got care and control

Out of the 29 mothers who wanted custody, care and control of their

TABLE 2
Type of proceedings

Separation	13
Divorce	14
Guardianship	2
Wardship	1
Care	2
Total numbers	32

children, 13 lost or gave up care and control, i.e. 45 per cent. Sixteen got care and control with either joint custody (nine) or sole custody (seven) i.e. 55 per cent.

Court hearings

Out of all these 29, only 11 got as far as disputing the case in court. The rest (18) came to agreement out of court, and these will be discussed later.

What happened to the lesbian mothers who attended at least one court hearing?

Seven mothers lost or gave up fighting for care and control after at least one court hearing. Four mothers got care and control.

Mothers who got care and control with at least one court hearing

TABLE 3
Settlement of disputes over custody

Number of women who had court hearings	11
Number of women who had no court hearings (settled out of court)	18
Total numbers	29

Reasons

One father agreed to give up care and control, during an adjournment in the hearing, if the mother would agree to joint custody, which she did. Whilst lesbianism was raised by the father's legal representatives in this case, it appears to have been disregarded by the court.

Another father did not actually want the children himself, but brought up lesbianism purely for reasons of revenge to create as much trouble as possible for the mother. A welfare report had been ordered for other reasons, and the father insisted that the mother's lesbianism was put in the welfare report. In this case, in a rare display of common sense, the judge remarked that his court was not the place for people to air their 'jealous and pernicious prejudices'. The father was reprimanded by the judge for attempting to ruin the mother's relationship with the children, particularly as he himself was not prepared to bring them up.

Another mother was awarded interim custody, care and control since the father was violent and she had an ouster injunction against him. However the judge made the condition that she should have no contact with her lover, and also made a supervision order. She subsequently decided to try and settle out of court in order to avoid another court hearing.

Only one woman won outright at a full hearing, despite the fact that the father actually wanted the children. However this case could be said to fall well within the 'default principle' since the father had no suitable accommodation, was unemployed, had a history of depressive illness and had a previous ouster injunction against him. A further disadvantage in the court's view was that he was 'foreign'. The mother, on the other hand, owned the house and worked in a professional job.

Welfare reports

There were three welfare reports ordered and all three recommended that the children should remain with their mothers. One mother was told, however, that if she got custody, the welfare officer would make certain that there was a supervision order on her, to ensure she did not have sex in front of the children.

In one case a psychiatrist's report was demanded by the father's side because of the mother's lesbianism. The psychiatrist's conclusion was that the mother had an immature sexuality. The mother who had to have a psychiatrist's report said that it was 'humiliating', and irrelevant since she only saw the psychiatrist for 40 minutes.

Status quo
All these mothers had the children living with them at the time of the dispute.

Age and sex
The ages of the children ranged from one to ten years at the time of the hearing and involved eight girls and two boys.

Supervision orders and conditions
One mother had a supervision order when she was granted interim custody. Another had to undertake to behave in a 'suitable' manner in front of the children, and not to involve the children in lesbian political activity, such as taking them on demonstrations.

Mothers who lost care and control and had at least one court hearing

Seven women lost care and control and had at least one court hearing. Out of these seven, lesbianism was raised as the main reason why the mother should not have care and control by the father's side in six cases. In the seventh the issue was decided on nationality grounds, although lesbianism would have been used if necessary. Three mothers gave up contesting after interim hearings; they gave the prejudice of the judge hearing the case and/or the prejudice of the welfare report as their reason. One women, who had been given interim custody with a supervision order, gave up because she did not want to have the children under such circumstances, nor did she wish to have to agree to a joint custody order with the father (the father had an ouster injunction against him for violence).

Welfare reports
There were five welfare reports, all of which focused on the mother's lesbianism as the main reason why she should not have the children.

Four women felt that their welfare officers were totally prejudiced against lesbians. One welfare officer told the mother that her children would grow up to be transvestites in their twenties without a father figure around. Another stated that the mother's lover was immature because she was a lesbian. Two assumed that where the mother lived with her partner, they would be acting out male and female roles, and that the mother's lover would take on the role of 'daddy'. One felt that if the mother was really concerned about her child, she should give up her lesbian relationship.

TABLE 4
Outcome of court hearings

Women who lost custody	7
Women who got custody	4
Total numbers	11

TABLE 5

Women who lost custody	*Type of hearings*
Withdrew after interim hearing	3
Went to full hearing	4
Total numbers	7

TABLE 6

Women who got custody	*Type of hearings*
Full hearing	1
Interim hearing	2
Father withdrew during adjournment	1
Total numbers	4

Psychiatric reports

There were psychiatric reports called for in two cases. In one case where three psychiatrists were used (two for the father's side) it was suggested that the mother's child, a boy, would have trouble growing up normal without a male model to emulate i.e. these two psychiatrists for the father used Freudian male identification theory.

In the other case, the psychiatrist was called because it was implied by the father's side that the mother was male. The psychiatrist did not however reach this conclusion and made no reference to the mother's sexuality.

Experience at court of the mothers who lost custody
One woman was asked by the judge whether she used 'appliances', another was asked whether her child saw her lover and her in bed together, and whether the child knew what they did. In two cases where the mother's lover appeared in court, one was asked whether she was 'the butch' in the relationship, another was asked where she slept when the children were there. The judge made comments in three cases. In one case the judge said the lover was an unsuitable parent substitute. In another, the judge asked the father to take both children (when the father had said he only wanted one) because of the mother's lesbianism.

In all the cases it was understood that lesbianism was the main reason why the mother was not awarded custody. This was variously expressed, but one of the most common reasons given was that the father and his new cohabitee could provide the appearance of a more normal family. There were five changes of status quo from mother to father; this included one change where the daughter had been living separately with the mother for six years, and another where a boy aged four had been living with the mother alone, for 2 years. (See table 7.)

The ages of the children of these mothers who lost custody ranged from 18 months to 11 years.

Who was expected to look after the children, where the mothers lost custody
Two mothers who lost custody through the courts said that the children would be looked after by the father's new wife or cohabitee; one stated that it would be a child minder, another said it would be the father's housekeeper, another said the father's mother. Only one mother said the father would look after the children. Therefore five out of the six mothers who answered the question stated that the children would not be looked after by the father himself. All the rest would be looked

after by strangers or other relatives.

Further, of the seven mothers who answered the question on the father's role in childcare, all said that the fathers had not done even as much as half the childcare when the parents had been living together. The majority of mothers stated that the fathers had done only a little childcare, such as putting the children to bed.

TABLE 7
Status quo situation of children of mothers who lost custody, and had court hearings

No. of children	Ages	Sex	Living situation at time of dispute
1	4	boy	Living with mother after she had separated from husband for 2 years
1	11	girl	Living with mother, after she had separated from father for 6 years
2	2,5	boys	Living with mother, after she had separated from father 4 months
2	4,5	girl, boy	Living with mother after she had separated from father one year
1	1½	boy	Living with mother after she had separated from father 6 months
4	all under 11	3 girls	Living with father, 3 months after mother had left home because of his violence
2	4,2	girls	One living with mother, one with father after separation 4 months

Total number of cases = 7

Behaviour of the father

One father got care and control with joint custody, despite a history of violence and a previous injunction against him. In addition, two mothers said that they had experienced violence from their husbands, as had their lovers. Two mothers stated that they had been sexually abused by the children's fathers, and one said that her lover had. Three said that the father had had other lovers whilst they were still living

TABLE 8
Father's share of child-caring tasks before separation

	None	A little	Half	More than half
Preparing meals	3	13	3	0
Feeding children	4	12	3	0
Shopping for food	4	12	3	0
Washing clothes/nappies	4	13	2	0
Bathing, putting to bed	1	16	2	0
Feeding babies, changing nappies	5	13	1	0
Buying children's clothes	8	11	0	0
Taking children to doctor, hospital, clinic	10	9	0	0

Total number of mothers who answered question = 19

with him. One father had never paid any maintenance whilst the mother had the child. Another, when he got care and control, refused to see to the medical treatment the child needed.

Mothers who settled out of court and lost custody

Six mothers settled out of court and lost care and control of their children. Three were advised by their solicitors that they stood no chance at all of getting custody. Out of these three, one was told by her solicitor that it would get in the newspapers if she fought the case. Another woman saw three different solicitors, two of whom told her she was 'diseased'. Two women who sought solicitors' advice were told that they might not even get access if they contested the case in court.

Two other women were told by their husbands that they would inform their employers they were lesbians; they therefore decided not to contest. One woman believed that because of society's attitudes she would never get custody of her children.

TABLE 9

Father's behaviour where mothers lost care and control (mother's experience)

2 Fathers had ouster injunctions against them for violence
3 Mothers said they had left home because of father's violence
3 Said father had been violent towards their lover
2 Mothers had experienced sexual abuse
1 Father looked at pornographic material
2 Fathers had never paid maintenance during separation when the mother had the child living with her
3 Fathers had other lovers

TABLE 10

Father's behaviour (all cases)

Violence

Towards mother	10
Ouster injunction	3
Towards mother's lover	6
Towards children	1

Sexual abuse

To mother	7
To children	0
To lover	2
Look at violent and pornographic material	6
Bring it into the home	4
Father had other lovers	10
Father paid maintenance on separation	4
Father did not pay maintenance on separation	5
Total numbers who replied to question	19

Lyn May

Living situation of the child/ren at the time of the dispute over custody

One woman was still living at home with her husband and children, whilst they negotiated over custody. Her children (both boys) were under five years old. The other five mothers had moved out of the matrimonial home without the children when custody negotiations began. Reasons for leaving the matrimonial home without the children varied. One woman said that she had left because her husband had become violent towards her when he discovered she was a lesbian: 'He forced me to leave home and told me I would lose the children, he would make sure of it.'

Another woman left home because of sexual pressures from her husband: 'The choice for me was to stay married and crack up under sexual pressure or to leave the marriage and the children. To leave and win the children seemed by then impossible, both in practical terms, a custody case, and nowhere to take them.'

Three other women said they would have taken the children with them, but had nowhere for them to live. For example one woman said that she had left the matrimonial home because her husband had refused to do so, and life had become unbearable, she had nowhere to take her two children.

Ages of children of mothers who felt forced to give up custody

There were five girls and nine boys involved. The ages of the children ranged from between the years of 2 and 11. Six children involved were aged six or under.

TABLE 11	
All mothers who lost custody	
After court hearings	7
With no court hearing	6
Total numbers	13

Living situation of the mother at the time of the dispute

Out of the seven women who lost custody and had at least one court hearing, four were living with a lover at the time the case came to court. In two cases it was stated by the court that the lover was not a suitable substitute parent. In one of the cases the welfare officer had stated that since the mother had not severed all connections with her lover, this showed a lack of commitment to her child.

One woman who also lost interim custody and then withdrew because of an unfavourable welfare report was, however, sharing a house with a heterosexual man. Another woman was sharing a house with several adults, and one was living on her own.

So whilst it would appear that the courts regard the mother living with a lover unfavourably, other living situations are not necessarily considered suitable either.

In the one fully contested case from our survey where the mother won custody, both she and the father were still living in the family home when the case came to court, and the mother owned the home.

In another case where the mother got interim custody, but with the condition that she had no contact with her lover, the mother and her children were staying with another family.

There was only one case where the mother was living with her lover and got custody.

Access for those mothers who lost care and control

Out of the 13 mothers who lost or gave up care and control, only three said they were satisfied with their access arrangements. Of those who settled out of court (six), four said that they were pressurised into agreeing to conditions being put on their access by the father. These conditions were all concerned with the mothers' lesbianism. Two were told not to 'flaunt' their lesbianism in front of the children or to make sure that they behaved in a suitable manner in front of the children. Three others could not have their lovers present when the children were there. In addition one had to agree not to tell her children she was a lesbian. One mother had to actually apply to court to get access as the father was refusing to let her have any access to her daughter. Similar conditions were imposed on those mothers who contested custody in the courts, e.g. two were ordered not to have their lovers present when they had the children, and two could not go to their child's school.

Type of access orders

Out of all the 13 mothers who lost care and control, 11 had defined access orders. Ten of these mothers felt that their defined access was too little.

Two women stated that their 'defined' access was dependent on their 'good behaviour' as stipulated by the father, i.e. one woman said that if she did anything to displease the father, she would not be allowed to see the children. Another mother had to travel over 130 miles to collect and return her child. One woman's defined access was only one day a month. The two women who had orders for reasonable access said that it was not frequent enough. One woman said that the father would cancel her access at a moment's notice, and it only amounted to two evenings a month anyway.

TABLE 12
Mothers who lost care and control
Those satisfied with access arrangements = 3
Those not satisfied with access arrangements = 10
Reasons
a) Her (defined) access was reduced. She also had to collect and return child over 130 miles. Access was originally every other weekend, meeting half way. This was subsequently reduced to half-terms and half the school holidays plus 3 weekends.
b) Access alternate weekends. The children are upset, mother had to see them at the father's house three days a week, before.
c) For the last two years if she displeased the father she would not see the children, now she still has to pacify him. For the last three years she could only see the children on Saturdays from 9–5. She now has staying access weekly.
d) Not flexible enough.
e) Defined access not frequent enough (half-term, half the holidays and two weekends a term). Seeing child more often is dependent on the father's 'goodwill' and the mother's 'good behaviour'.
f) 'Reasonable (undefined) access.' Father will cancel access at a moment's notice (2 evenings a month).
g) Defined access – 10 weeks a year. Has to travel several hundred miles to collect the child.
h) Alternate weekends and alternate holidays. Not satisfied but no reasons given.
i) Not frequent enough (only one day a month).
j) 'Reasonable' access – not frequent enough.

Women who got care and control out of court

Twelve women were finally able to negotiate care and control without having to contest the case in court. In virtually all these cases the father had begun the custody dispute not because he really wanted the children, but because he wanted to create as much trouble as possible for the mother.

Out of the 12 women who were able to negotiate care and control, six got sole custody, and six got joint custody.

Those mothers who got sole custody did so for a variety of reasons. One father who began contesting custody only wanted to have custody of his son and not his two daughters. When he was told he might get all three if he brought up lesbianism in court, he ceased to contest. Another father ceased to contest when his girl friend decided she did not want to live with the children. Another father disappeared abroad half way through the proceedings, and did not return. One father withdrew, when the mother agreed not to cite his violent behaviour as grounds for divorce. Another father only began proceedings when he discovered his wife was a lesbian, nine years after he had left her. He had only seen his daughter twice a year in all that time. He withdrew when he was refused legal aid, and had been advised by a child psychologist that moving the daughter to his home would do more damage than her mother's lesbianism.

All these women had their children living with them at the time of the dispute, and the ages of the children involved ranged from two to 12 years. There were four boys and six girls.

TABLE 13

Conditions placed on access

Of those who lost care and control, conditions were placed on access in 7 cases.

a) Not to go to his school, and lover not to accompany child.

b) Not to flaunt lesbianism.

c) Not to mention lesbianism, or to have lover there.

d) To behave in a suitable manner in front of the children.

e) Lover not to be present.

f) Not to go to the school.

g) Not to mention lesbianism.

h) Not to sleep with lover, when children are there.

Joint custody with care and control to the mother

Six women were advised by their solicitors to agree to joint custody so that lesbianism would not be brought up in a contested case. Out of these one case is not yet resolved. Joint custody was therefore used as a bargaining tool to pacify the father. All of these women stated that they were unhappy about the joint custody agreement, and still felt that they were being controlled by the father. They believed that unless they did what he wanted he would go to court and contest custody, using the issue of lesbianism against them.

One woman said about the sort of control the father had over her: 'It is as simple and terrible as not being free. I am not able to be as honest and open with my child, my friends or my acquaintances about my life.' Another woman stated that she had to pretend to have an 'amicable relationship' with the father over arrangements and access, because if she stepped out of line he could always go back to court, and get care and control.

Another mother said she wished she had not agreed to joint custody as the father uses it to 'tell her what to do'. This same man had been violent towards her lover and shown the children violent and pornographic videos when he had access. However she stated: 'I know that he could go back to court at any time, and he would probably win. I am still worried that this could happen.'

Another mother said that she worried that the children might be ordered to go into care if she fought a contested case as the father had a history of mental illness. She had therefore agreed to joint custody in order to keep the case out of court.

TABLE 14
All mothers who got care and control, with joint custody or sole custody out of court

Sole custody to mother	6
Care and control to mother, with joint custody	6
Total numbers	12

Mothers who had care and control: problems with the fathers' access

Out of all the mothers who got care and control of their children (16) only two said that they had no problems over the fathers' access. Problems ranged from threats of violence and kidnapping to the threat of going to court, and bringing up lesbianism if the mother did not agree to what the father wanted. In the situation where the mother agreed care and control out of court, the threat of going to court and bringing up lesbianism was usually enough to force the mother to agree to more access than she would otherwise have done. For example, one father demanded all the weekends and holidays for his access times, another demanded three days a week access, imposing virtual shared care and control on the mother. Another father, whilst threatening to go to court if the mother did not increase his access, frequently left the child with his own mother.

Another mother who had been awarded sole custody by the court had had continual problems over access periods with children being returned late, and never knowing whether they would be returned at all. In the end this father's access was terminated by the court after he had kidnapped the children. Three women had experienced threats of violence or actual violence during access times, and this had only been resolved by using third parties to deliver and collect the children from the father. One mother had had to go to the police several times, to escape her husband's violence during access periods.

Care orders

Two women had problems with local authority social services intervention, one resulting in an actual care order, and the children being removed from the mother's home into care because of her lesbianism. In both cases intervention came about through the children's school. In one case a girl was sexually assaulted at school, and the school brought in social services. It was implied by the school and social services that the child had been assaulted at home, because her mother was a lesbian. Social services threatened the mother with a place of safety order on the child, but then withdrew it if the mother and child would agree to child guidance. Neither the school nor the police did anything to look for the man who had sexually assaulted the child.

In the other case the school brought in social services because one of the mother's two children was being teased about his mother's lesbianism. The mother had been living with her lover in an openly lesbian relationship. As a result a care order was made on the children in the mother's absence. There was later a full court hearing, and it was decided that the children should remain in the care of the local authority. The reasons given by the court were 'hostility' in the neighbourhood, and 'hostility' towards one of the children at school, because of the mother's lesbianism. There was a social enquiry report, which was unfavourable to the mother and her partner's household, but an independent child guidance report described both children as perfectly balanced, happy, and healthy. Since the children went into care, the mother was allowed access once every three weeks, and the mother's lover was only allowed to see the children for five minutes under supervision. It was felt that the social services could not bear to see a 'happy lesbian household, that worked'.

Thus instead of the school combating the anti-lesbian and heterosexist attitudes of its students, it was considered better that the children should be removed from their mother. This is the most extreme example of prejudice that has emerged from this survey.

Problems for women who had no dispute over custody

Out of the four women who had no dispute over custody, one woman stated that her husband had not known she was a lesbian at the time of her divorce, so he had not disputed custody. However she felt that because of this she had to remain 'firmly in the closet', even to her children, as they were too young to keep a secret, and she was afraid that if her ex-husband found out he would try to get the children. Another woman was not a lesbian at the time of her divorce, but subsequently felt restrained about being open about her lesbianism for the same reasons. Her child, who knows she is a lesbian, visits her father regularly, and has to operate under the same restraints in case the father finds out.

Another mother, whilst she had no problems over getting custody, was involved in a dispute with the father over increased access, and felt that she had to agree, in case he brought up her lesbianism. Only one woman said she had no problems over custody or access, but that was because the father did not want the child.

Other discrimination against lesbian mothers

School and Nursery

Ten mothers said they had experienced problems because of their lesbianism at their child's school. Some experienced hostility from teachers, others who had lost custody were refused access to the school and lovers or friends were excluded from the school or from picking up the children.

One mother said she was treated as a 'problem family' by the school, another said her daughter had become a school refuser, and the teachers blamed the mother's lesbianism rather than the other pupils'

TABLE 15
Problems at school or nursery

Number of mothers who stated they had problems	10
Out of these:	
Number of mothers who were excluded from the school (all had lost care and control)	3
Number of mothers who experienced hostility towards lesbianism	7
Sub-total	10
Mothers who stated they made sure the school didn't know	3
Total numbers	13

These figures cannot be taken as a true representation of anti-lesbian attitudes and practices by schools, even in this survey, as many lesbian mothers do not tell the school that they are lesbians.

heterosexism. Two mothers said that the school was far more supportive to the father, because she and her lover were lesbians and
feminists. Three mothers who had lost care and control said they had
been excluded from going to the school altogether.

One mother stated that she had problems in terms of 'heterosexist
attitudes', i.e. denial of her lesbian lifestyle at her child's nursery.

In addition to these 10 mothers, three others said they took care that
the school didn't find out about their lesbianism.

Neighbours
Two mothers said that they had experienced hostility and harassment
from neighbours. One said that she had experienced harassment and
anti-lesbian abuse from young men and boys on her estate, and
anti-lesbian graffiti had been painted on her walls.

Police
Three women said that they had experienced problems with the police.
Two experienced anti-lesbian hostility when they needed help in
getting their children returned after their father had overrun the access
period. One woman said she was harassed by police in cars, because
they knew she was a lesbian.

Health services
Two women said they had experienced discrimination from the health
services. One said that health visitors and doctors assumed that a
(self-insemination) child was handicapped because of the self-
insemination. Another said that her medical records had listed her
lesbianism as a medical problem.

Welfare reports summary
Out of the mothers who went to court and lost care and control, five
had welfare reports. Three said they felt their welfare officers were
biased against them because they were lesbians. In each case the
officers had given lesbianism as the reason why the mother should not
have care and control in the report. One said there was no bias
expressed against lesbianism, but against feminism.

Some of the verbal attitudes expressed by welfare officers were:

lesbians have immature personalities; lesbians have stereotypical butch
and femme relationships; lesbians have sex in front of the children;
children of lesbians would grow up to be transvestites; children of
lesbians would be better off growing up in 'normal family' environ-
ments.

On the other hand, in cases where the mothers had welfare reports
and got care and control, all three said they thought the welfare
officers were not biased against them as lesbians, and two said that
their welfare officers had not regarded it as relevant. Another mother
whose case is not yet resolved said that her welfare officer was not
biased.

TABLE 16
Results of welfare reports where lesbianism was known

Welfare Reports	No.	Bias	No Bias
Mothers who lost care and control	5	4	1
Mothers who got care and control	3		3
Not resolved	1		1
Totals	9	4	5

The legal profession
Eight women out of the 26 who answered the questions on legal
representatives felt that their solicitors were biased against them
because they were lesbians. In three cases as discussed earlier, this
prevented women from taking their fight for custody any further. One
woman who experienced such bias emphasised how important it is 'to
find a solicitor who does not believe it is wrong to be a lesbian'. Four
others, all of whom lost or gave up custody after court hearings, felt
that their solicitors' prejudice towards lesbianism had not helped their
case. One of these women felt that her solicitor had 'colluded with the
father'. Another again emphasised how important it was to find
solicitors who are sympathetic to lesbian mothers and explained how a
poor solicitor can 'knock the fight right out of you'. Another woman
said that her solicitor's 'naivety' about the issues had affected the way
in which her case was conducted.

Eight women stated that their solicitors lacked knowledge of lesbian custody disputes and three that they did not know whether their solicitors knew anything about it or not. Three women changed their solicitors when they found out they had no knowledge or experience, and were able to find other solicitors who did.

Four women who lost custody felt that their solicitors' lack of knowledge and experience had affected their case negatively. Four women felt that their solicitors' previous experience and knowledge had been positively helpful. One woman who had regained her right to access, which the father had terminated on the grounds of her lesbianism, described her solicitor as excellent, another said that it was important that her solicitor had actually come across lesbian mothers before. Two women also stated that it had been important that their solicitors showed support and understanding in the situation they faced, and recognised the emotional stress of a long-drawn-out lesbian custody battle. Others, however, complained of their solicitors' failure to keep them informed about what was happening which had added to the stressful situation.

Thirteen women stated that they were affected by their solicitors' advice. In six cases this was to settle for joint custody with care and control to the mother, in order to keep the case out of court. In three cases the advice was not to go for custody at all, but to ask for access only. In the other three cases it was to fight for sole custody and hope that the father would cease to contest, and in one case to fight for joint custody through the courts. One woman felt that her solicitor refused to understand that joint custody would involve too many controls on her.

Barristers

Barristers appeared to be in general ignorant about lesbian custody issues, according to the women in our survey. Out of the six women who had barristers, only one thought that her barrister (a woman) was helpful. Other comments about barristers were 'he treated lesbianism as a bit of a joke', 'he was apologetic about lesbianism', and 'he was confused about the issues'. Another woman felt her barrister totally misrepresented her in court.

Class, race and financial situation

Out of the 36 questionnaires returned, 20 women answered the question 'Do you think your case was affected by your race/class/ financial situation? If yes, please state how'.

Class

A small number of women (four) felt that class had affected their access to the legal profession and also their knowledge of the legal system. One working-class woman stated:

> 'Class is obviously an issue for me. If I'd mixed with people in the legal profession I could have found out that lesbians lost their children. He (her ex-husband) is middle-class, has money, powerful family and friends, and didn't have to pay for information from solicitors, he just asked around.'

Three women felt their access to the legal profession had been easier, because they were middle class. One of them felt that she was treated better because she was a teacher, another that her middle-class position meant that her solicitor asked her fewer questions.

Financial situation and class

Both working-class and middle-class women felt that their cases had been affected by their financial situation. Two middle-class women felt that their financial independence had allowed them to come to an agreement out of court for joint custody, care and control to them, and they did not have to ask for maintenance. Having to demand maintenance might have meant a court dispute, where their lesbianism could have been used against them.

Three middle-class women stated that their poor financial situation compared with the father's had not helped their case. All these women lost custody. One middle-class woman, who was in a better financial situation than the father and owned their previously shared home, felt this had helped her as far as getting custody was concerned. She felt that if the situation had been reversed (where the father was better off) she would not have got custody in guardianship proceedings.

On the other hand, two middle-class women who lost custody had at least as good material and financial positions as the fathers, and stated that they felt these circumstances had not affected their case, lesbianism was the crucial factor.

Two working-class women felt that class and lack of financial resources had affected their case. One woman said that since she was from a working-class family, with no financial resources, she had no 'financial safety net' to fall back on. Therefore she had not even contested custody, since she had nowhere to take the children when she left the matrimonial home. Homelessness was particularly a problem.

Another stated that her poor financial situation had meant she was in a weaker position than the father, and therefore she kept the dispute out of court and agreed to what he wanted.

Race
Only one woman stated in the questionnaire that she was black, and her case was as yet unresolved at the time of filling out her questionnaire, so she did not know whether this would have any effect.

Another stated that the fact that her husband was a 'foreigner' and could speak little English had gone against him in court and in dealing with the legal profession. She had won custody.

DISCUSSION

Over half the lesbian mothers in our survey who were in dispute over custody (18) avoided contesting their cases through the courts, because they believed or were legally advised that they had little chance of winning.

In a few cases (three) women did not even take legal advice, as they understood that they would have no chance of keeping their children, given 'society's' hostility towards them.

Whilst one of these women gave up custody in 1976, another believed she had no hope at all as recently as 1982. Of those women who took legal advice, three were told that because of 'the attitudes of the courts' in this country, they stood no chance of getting custody. All these women were given this advice in the last four years.

Other women (six) avoided going through a contested case by coming to a joint custody agreement, whereby they kept care and control but had joint custody with the father. All of these women stated that they felt pressurised into making a joint custody agreement, and would have preferred sole custody. However, because of the threat of the father using lesbianism against them in court, they felt forced to agree; most of them were following the advice of their solicitors who also felt they would lose a lesbian custody battle. Of the women who went through at least one court hearing (11), two were awarded joint custody and one withdrew after the interim hearing and agreed to settle for joint custody. Thus 75 per cent of the women in our sample who had care and control also had joint custody with the father. This figure is much higher than is quoted for heterosexual mothers (between 8 per cent and 10 per cent), most of whom get sole custody.

Many of the women felt that far from the joint custody arrangement being 'in the best interests of the children', the fathers were using it to control and interfere in the women's lives.

In examining the individual cases of the women who did get sole custody (six), it became clear that the fathers did not really want the children, but had started the dispute in order to create trouble for the mother – what may be described as the revenge motive. One father even disappeared abroad half way through proceedings. The revenge motive also became apparent in the one case where the father did not want the children himself, but insisted that the mother's lesbianism was brought to the attention of the judge and the welfare officer.

In the one fully contested case where the mother got custody (1981) and where the father actually wanted the children, it became clear that the mother was in a much better financial and material situation than the father. So the contest was by no means equal. Her case was also assisted by a favourable welfare report.

The effect of the welfare report in the contested cases was considerable. Where the welfare officer had expressed negative attitudes towards lesbianism and the effects of lesbianism on children, the mothers lost custody.

The effects of the psychiatric reports were less clear, but tend to support the hypothesis that judges use psychiatric opinion that fits in with their own views. Whilst there were only three psychiatric reports in our survey, in two cases the judge chose to ignore their conclusions.

Controls on mothers

In the few cases where mothers did get custody through the courts, controls were still exerted by the imposition of conditions. One mother who got interim custody had a supervision order imposed on her, as well as an order that she and the children were to have no contact with her lover whatsoever.

In other cases where the mother lost custody, she had to agree to conditions imposed on her access either by the father's solicitor or by the courts. For example, one mother was ordered not to have her lover present when she saw the children; another woman had to agree not to tell her children she was a lesbian. Only in one case, where the mother was being refused access by the father because of her lesbianism, did the court regard her sexuality as irrelevant.

Similar controls were exerted by the schools, where mothers had lost care and control: some schools would not allow the mothers access or refused to communicate with them.

Controls were also put on mothers who had come to an agreement out of court. Several of those who had been granted access were subjected to violent behaviour and personal abuse from the fathers, which they put up with for fear of the threat of lesbianism being brought up and used against them. Women who got custody either because they didn't say they were lesbians or because they had become lesbians after their divorce felt similar controls on their lives.

In this situation, because custody is never final, their main fear was that if the father found out they were lesbians, he could apply to the court for a change of custody. Thus these women had to remain extremely closeted, and in one case the mother was unable to tell the children she was a lesbian.

Those women who opted to fight an actual custody battle through the courts found the whole process painful and humiliating. As in the appeal cases discussed earlier the mothers' sexuality became the focus of the case, rather than their parenting abilities or the fact that they had been the main carers of their children. Little attention was paid to the father's previous experience as a carer or his suitability as a parent, or the role model he might provide for the children. In the vast majority of the cases in our survey, this went unquestioned. Only in two cases was it assumed that he would do any childcaring anyway. In all the other cases the expectation was that someone else would look after the children. Nor was there any questioning of the father's behaviour or the effect this might have on the children.

In two cases, women had found themselves involved in a lesbian custody dispute when they had applied for ouster injunctions. Other mothers were forced to leave home because of the father's violence or sexual abuse. However, the father's violent behavior became insignificant in the light of a much worse 'crime' in the eyes of the courts – the mother's lesbianism. Nor were other aspects of the father's behaviour considered to be significant; even where he failed in his traditional role of provider, i.e. the failure to pay maintenance. The concern of the courts appeared to be that of providing heterosexual models and the appearance of a normal family, however unsuitable or questionable this might be in reality, and regardless of whether this might be most appropriate to the welfare of the child. As in the cases discussed earlier, it is assumed that it must be better for the child to live in a heterosexual family, and that fathers must be good for children.

Where fathers made unfounded allegations against mothers, particularly in terms of parenting abilities, the judges, magistrates and in some cases welfare officers, tended to believe them rather than the mothers. It was as if, once the mothers had stated they were lesbians, they came to be regarded as 'inadequate' or 'unfit' in other areas, as well as the sexual.

These attitudes are no doubt related to what is regarded as women's traditional role, as a wife, providing a man with children, and being dependent on men. Once women step out of this role they become 'criminalised'. This was emphasised by one woman, who said that she and her lover were made to feel ' as if they were the worst, most despicable criminals in the land', and by another who stated 'I am a good mother and a loving mother, but because I am a lesbian living with a lesbian for some odd reason I am not capable. What a crazy system.'

In this sense the legal system may also be seen as punishing women for stepping out of the traditional role assigned to them. One woman stated:

> 'I was amazed to find for the first time in my life that because I had done something to "deviate" from the norms of society, I had no power at all. I was surprised that the feelings, wishes and welfare of my children and what were best for them was not taken into account at all. The object of the exercise seemed to be to punish me for doing wrong, by depriving me of my children. They succeeded.'

Ideal motherhood

A few women gave up fighting for custody, rather than having to go on proving they were ideal mothers. One woman who didn't have custody stated: 'I love my children very much and would like to play a major part in their lives. It's just that as a lesbian I have learned to value myself far more than I used to, and consequently motherhood is not enough as an end in itself. I want to be a lesbian mother on my own terms.'

On the other hand, the strain of being separated from their children was extremely great for some women. Two women said that losing their children had caused them serious illness and had devastated their lives. One woman felt forced to return to the matrimonial home after losing interim custody and receiving an unfavourable welfare report at a subsequent hearing.

Racism

It would appear that the majority of women who replied to the survey were white, therefore no conclusions can be drawn from this sample of the effects of living in a racist society on black and ethnic minority lesbian mothers. In addition the orientation of the survey may not have reflected the particular discrimination that black lesbians have to face in relation to the law, the police and social services particularly. Racist and sexist immigration rules make it doubly difficult for black and ethnic minority women in relation to getting custody of their children.

Conclusion

The results of this survey show discrimination against lesbian mothers at all institutional levels, including the courts, welfare officers, and the legal profession, as well as teachers and social services, and the medical profession.

There appears to have been little change of attitude by the courts over an eight-year period, from 1976 to 1984, at least from this sample. Where lesbian mothers have 'won custody' their lives are still controlled and invaded by the imposition of conditions and supervision orders.

15
Lesbian Custody Cases in the USA

In the USA, child custody law (as well as other areas of law) varies from state to state. Almost every state has statutes which define the legal criteria to be applied in determining child custody cases. However there is one overriding principle which is adhered to in all states, namely 'the best interests of the child'. This is of course akin to the English requirement that all cases be decided on the basis that the welfare of the child is the first and paramount consideration.

State court rulings do not bind other states' courts and do not necessarily bind another court in the same state. The judge has only to review precedents made by higher courts so judges are still left with a wide discretion in considering what they believe to be in the best interests of the child.

The factors which are taken into consideration in US courts before awarding custody to one or other parent are similar to those in England but there are additional factors when it comes to a case where the mother is a lesbian. Some of the questions raised by the court in considering placing the child with a lesbian mother may include:
1. Whether her lesbianism has any effect on the child
2. Whether her lesbianism had made her an 'unfit' parent
3. The future effect of the mother's lesbianism on the child
4. The mother's general moral character, conduct and disposition
5. Age and sex of the child

Other considerations include whether homosexuality is unlawful in the state in which the case is heard and whether the mother lives with a lover.

Some of the above questions show that unlike English courts, the US courts at least seem to consider that lesbianism in itself is not a ground for denying a lesbian mother custody of her child. There is a move towards a situation where if it cannot be shown that the mother's lesbianism has an adverse effect on the child, then the mother should not be denied custody or access to the child. There must therefore be a connection between the mother's lesbianism and the welfare of the child.

The case of *Bezio v Patenaude* (1980)[1] decided that 'a finding that a parent is unfit to further the welfare of the child' must be based on 'parental behaviour which adversely affects the child. The state may not deprive parents of custody of the children simply because their household fails to meet the ideals approved by the community . . . or simply because the parents embrace ideologies or pursue a lifestyle at odds with the average.' The court accepted the opinion of an 'expert' witness (professor of psychology and clinical psychologist) who said that a mother's sexual preference in itself is irrelevant to a consideration of her parenting skills.

This view was upheld in the case of *Doe v Doe* (1981)[2] where an appeal court overruled a decision of a lower court which had held that every lesbian mother is an unfit parent.

Another case decided that although consideration should be given to the fact that the mother had a relationship with another woman, this relationship had no adverse effect on the children nor was there any evidence that it would do so in the future (*Madeiros v Madeiros* (1982)).[3]

In *Smith v Smith* (1978)[4] the Michigan Circuit Court reversed a decision and awarded custody of a young boy to his mother: 'if two female homosexuals can give that kind of care, it matters not that they are lesbian, nor does it matter if the child is male or female. Lesbianism is a choice, not an abnormality.'

The positive decisions from the US courts also confirm that a court must consider *all* the evidence in a case and award custody in the light of that evidence. Lesbianism should not be singled out as being the dominant or only factor. The court in the case of *MP v SP* (1979)[5] rejected a father's claim that the mother's sexual orientation might cause embarrassment to her daughters and said that there must be some factual basis for deciding not to give custody to the mother, and that pure speculation about future harm was an inappropriate basis for making a decision against the mother. It made an analogy with an interracial marriage situation and said: 'Neither the prejudice of the small community in which they live nor the curiosity of their peers about the Defendant's sexual nature will be abated by the change of custody. Hard facts must be faced. These are matters which Courts cannot control . . .' The court was of the opinion that the girls would be better equipped to make their own judgements and deal with the possible difficulties if they stayed with their mother, whereas removal from the mother would instill in them a sense of shame for her.

A similar analogy was made in *K v K* (1976)[6]: 'A heterosexual living with a partner of the opposite sex but of a different race would be equally likely to suffer from negative community reactions and this would be visited upon the children.'

Although US courts are in general more 'open' in considering custody cases where the mother is a lesbian, there are still a number of biased rulings against lesbians. For example, in a situation where the mother's lover was living with her, the court decided that it was likely the child would have serious adjustment problems. In the case of *Jacobson v Jacobson* (1981)[7] an appeal court overruled a lower court which had granted the mother custody, stating that because of the attitudes of today's society, because the mother had a live-in lover, and because of the lack of legal recognition on the status of homosexual relationships, the best interests of the children would be better served by giving custody to the father.

In these cases the mother is usually granted access, better known in the US as 'visitation'. However, strict conditions are often attached to visitation orders, and the most common are:

1. The mother's lover is totally excluded from contact with the children (*Distefano v Distefano* (1978));[8]
2. Visits are only allowed in the day-time and at places where no other homosexuals are present, including the mother's lover (in *Re Jane B* (1976)[9] and *Loudon v Loudon* (1971));[10]
3. The mother's lover never to stay overnight and to have no physical contact with the mother (*Irish v Irish* (1981));[11]
4. One weekend a month only, and the mother's lover must be away (*L v D* (1982)).[12]

It is not therefore unusual for a lesbian mother to be faced with the choice of living either with her lover or with her children. The burden of proof also appears to fall on the mother to show that being a lesbian does not render her an unfit parent. To do this she often, as in England, has to call 'expert' evidence (e.g. psychologists and psychiatrists) to testify to her ability as a parent and her general mental state as well as to assess any effect of her lesbianism on the children. An expert is often used to 'educate' the courts, for example in the case of *Belmont v Belmont* (1980)[13] the court heard evidence from a psychiatrist specialising in problems of human sexuality and psycho-sexual development in children.

Campaigners and lawyers in the US have also looked at wider implications of the general bias against lesbian mothers in custody cases. In doing so, they have drawn on the rights given to individuals under the constitution and the possible breach of those rights.

There are two main rights applicable here, first the right of freedom of speech and freedom of association (which is basic to the First Amendment of the constitution). The association involved would be the association of the lesbian mother with other lesbians and it can be argued that denial or limitation of custody to a lesbian mother on the grounds of her sexual preference contravenes that right. The state is not allowed to deny or limit these rights unless it can prove the mother's lesbianism is detrimental to the child's welfare.

The second right under the constitution is the right of privacy. The right of privacy should protect a lesbian mother from interference in childraising, choice of sexuality, and lifestyle. A lesbian mother's interests in having custody of her child, in non-interference in child-rearing, and in her own sexual preference are fundamental and are protected by this right. Unless the state can prove that the mother's lesbian conduct is detrimental to the child's welfare, the state should not be able to interfere in the mother-child relationship.

Other rights which can be invoked include the right to 'due process' i.e. the right to a fair trial, where a lesbian mother shall not be prejudiced as unfit; and the right to 'equal protection' which orders that when the state makes a distinction between two types of people for the purpose of granting or denying some right or privilege, there must be some rational basis and justification for the distinction.

These basic principles of constitutional rights are still being tried and tested in US courts. However in *Clements v Bennet* (1973),[14] a judge who disagreed with his colleagues said:

'Where neglect, abuse, or mistreatment in sòme manner is absent, the State has no right to enquire into what a parent teaches (her) child, or with whom a parent allows (her) child to associate . . . These are fundamental family rights, protected by the Common Law and our Bill of Rights, free from government intrusion. Freedom to think, teach and express, freedom to association with other persons or classes of persons with varying degrees of morality and philosophy . . . and freedom to adopt a lifestyle that may not have the approval of the majority; all of these . . . freedoms exist even more emphatically within the family or the parent-child relationship . . . the State cannot intrude upon or disrupt this relationship by asserting a different moral standard, conceived by judges, that must be adhered to.'

Despite the fact that there is no constitution in this country, there is the European Convention of Human Rights, which could possibly be invoked in lesbian custody cases. Further, the principles used in deciding custody cases in some American states, such as the requirement to prove rather than to assume that lesbianism produces a negative effect on the child's upbringing, could be applied in this country.

Following on from this is the principle in some states that a parent cannot be deprived of custody simply because the household fails to meet the ideals approved of by the community, or fails to conform to the average.

16
Lesbian Custody Cases in Australia

This information on lesbian custody cases in Australia is taken from a report on 'Homosexual Parenting' produced for the Family Court of Australia. In Australia, as in England, the court is directed to treat the 'welfare of the child' as the paramount consideration in all child custody cases.[1]

The Family Court of Australia dealt with 18 custody disputes involving lesbian mothers during the period 1976–80. Nine of these mothers were granted or retained custody, and nine lost custody. Of the nine who won custody, four had conditions put on them (e.g. no displays of 'sexual affection' in front of the children) and five had no conditions put on them. Of the nine mothers who lost custody, two had conditions put on their access, and six did not. In the ninth case, the children were put into care and the mother was given several conditions to fulfil before she could get custody back. The outcome of this case is not known.

It is evident from these cases that the results depend mainly upon the attitudes of the individual judges, as is the case in England. Although the assumptions and fears about lesbianism tend to be uniform, the judgments in similar cases vary considerably depending upon the attitude of the judge. For instance in the case of G (1979)[2] the mother lived in an open lesbian relationship with her lover. The judge accepted the opinion of the family counsellor that the lesbian relationship appeared to have no adverse effect upon the child, and that there was no evidence of any harm being caused to a child through being brought up in a homosexual household. The mother was given custody without conditions.

In the case of T(1980)[3], however, the wife was accused of being less discreet in her relationship than she made out. In the face of contradictory evidence from a psychologist and a psychiatrist, the judge decided to award custody to the father, even though the mother had better accommodation to offer. The main reason he gave was his own fear of negative community attitudes towards lesbians.

Another reflection on judges is that although the Australian judges may appear to be more liberal than their English counterparts, their final decisions often belie the liberality of their words. For instance, in the case of *Campbell v Campbell* (1974)[4], Judge Bright made the following statement which has been frequently quoted since: 'The days are gone when the courts will disqualify a woman from the role of parent merely because she had engaged or is engaging in some form of extra-marital sex, be it heterosexual or homosexual.' The father in this case was considered an unsuitable parent, with inadequate accommodation and proposals for looking after the children, and the mother was awarded custody. Her custody, however, was on condition that she did not sleep with her lover overnight, or engage in any 'acts of a sexual nature' in the presence of the children or anyone else who might report these acts to them. The children were also to be seen by a child psychiatrist annually.

Other conditions imposed by the courts on lesbian mothers include: 'not to engage in any overt displays of a sexual nature, in the presence of the children and no public display of affection between the women' W (1978)[5]; 'that the wife refrain from any act or word which would reasonably be calculated to suggest that she or any friend of hers is a lesbian' Cartwright (1977).[6]

These conditions show very clearly that the courts consider lesbianism as something undesirable to be kept a secret from the children and society as a whole. They also reflect the two main arguments which are used, without evidence to support them, against lesbian mothers having custody of their children, namely, that the children will be corrupted or psychologically damaged in some way by their mother's lesbianism; and that the children will suffer from social stigma. These two arguments were brought out clearly in the English Appeal case of *Re P* (a minor)'. There is no mention anywhere of the detrimental effect hiding her lesbianism might have on the mother, or lover, or the effects that this might have on the children and their relationships with them.

The good news is that all these conditions were imposed on lesbian mothers during the period 1974–78. In the period from 1978–80, although there was no increase in the percentage of cases won, there were no more conditions imposed on either custody or access.

The first case in which no conditions were imposed after 1978 was the case of *Schmidt v Schmidt* (1979)[8] which concerned a 14-year-old girl who was living with her father but wanted to live with her mother. The father presented the risks to the child in terms of sexual advances by the mother's lover; the adverse effect of the mother's homosexual friends; the absence of a male figure; the fear of the child becoming homosexual. These are all typical arguments brought up in the courts against lesbianism. Fortunately Judge Elisabeth Evatt found that *none* of these factors presented any risk to the child, and gave the following opinion:

> 'The ordinary observations of life would lead me to the view that one lesbian relationship could not necessarily be judged by another. There must be many variations in the personalities involved, in the intensity of feeling in the social relationship with other persons, male and female, heterosexual and homosexual. It could be a mistake to regard a person's sexual proclivities as the dominating trait of their personality as if it was something that occupied their sole attention and thoughts. The difficult task always confronting the Family Court is that of searching for the quality of relationships and in assessing the personality and character concerned in custody and access matters.'[9]

The second main argument used against lesbian mothers having custody of their children is that of the social stigma the children *might* suffer. This is one which crops up again and again in both English and Australian custody cases, and is often the *only* reason given for denying lesbians custody.

In the case of *P v P* (1976)[10], the mother was awarded custody, but the judge made the following remark about societal attitudes, which has been used in other cases as an argument against giving lesbian mothers custody: 'the community in general is still sufficiently old-fashioned to view with disfavour and even with abhorrence, unnatural sexual acts – whether between male and female, or male and male, or female and female, and whether they be illegal or not'. This was unreported so there are no details available about the father or whether there was any 'suitable' alternative to the mother having custody.

In the case of *Spry* (1977)[11] the judge was worried about the effects on the two girls (aged seven and ten) of growing up in a 'lesbian milieu' despite the fact that 50 per cent of the wife's friends were heterosexual, and was concerned again about community attitudes. Both children were subjected to psychological tests and the psychologist's conclusion was that 'it is by no means certain that a lesbian environment is likely to influence the girls towards deviant behaviour'. However the judge was not convinced, and awarded custody to the father. Mrs S and her lover were granted access with conditions.

In the case of *Cartwright* (1977)[12] referred to earlier, the judge awarded custody to the mother because the eldest child was 14 and wanted to live with her. He recognised that there was a very close and loving relationship between her and the children, and decided that her love for them would 'minimize any chance of her behaviour harming them'. However he gave the mother custody on condition that her lesbianism should be kept *hidden from the children*.

In the case of *R* (1979)[13] custody of three girls was given to their mother. The father was unemployed and had no accommodation for them. Judge Pauley made the following remark about the possible social stigma the children might come across:

'Having taken into consideration also the question of any disadvantage which the children are likely to suffer at school or in their society among their peers because of their mother's relationship, I have come to the conclusion that this disadvantage is not likely to outweigh the advantages which they will continue to have living with a caring and sensitive mother with whom they have lived all their lives. There is no evidence before me that they are subject to taunts at school or elsewhere because of the conduct of their mother and I think that sometimes too much emphasis can be placed on that possibility in a rapidly changing world.' Hopefully this kind of attitude will be shown more often.

In the case of *PC and PR* (1979)[14], and *Tiffin* (1979)[15], two lesbian mothers were not awarded custody because it was assumed that their sons were psychologically at risk through living in an all-female household. Some typical, yet contradictory myths about lesbians were also brought out in these cases. In the first (*PC and PR*) the mother was described as 'immature' and 'emotional'. In the second (*Tiffin*) the mother was critically described as 'intellectual' and 'unemotional'. This despite the fact that the court had been told that she and her lover had deliberately adopted a cool attitude in court in order not to be judged as 'too emotional'. However, the husband's violence towards the mother and her lover was treated as something natural and to be expected. In both these cases the lovers were cast by the court into the role of 'dominating' and 'aggressive' lesbians who were leading the mothers astray. This is a frequent stereotype of the lovers of lesbian mothers. It is also evident from the constant use of psychologists and psychiatrists that lesbianism is still seen by the courts as a mental sickness, or at least both the cause and the result of psychological disturbances.

The myths and prejudices used against lesbian mothers in the English courts are also prevalent in Australia, and the majority of the cases won by mothers are won by default, i.e. because of the father's unsuitability. However, there have been some encouraging developments in Australia. This is evidenced by the recent, more enlightened attitudes of some judges, e.g. Chief Judge Evatt and Senior Judge Pawley, and the fact that no conditions were imposed on custody or access after 1978.

Since 1977 two substantial reports have appeared containing information relevant to lesbian custody cases. One was a Royal Commission set up to enquire into and report upon matters relating to Homosexuality and Homosexual Parenting to which a number of well-researched and reasoned papers were submitted, including papers from Chief Judge Evatt and the Gay Task Force. The other was the Royal Commission on Human Relationships which revealed that, although there are still some firmly held views against homosexuality, the tide of community opinion has definitely turned.

17
Possible Changes and Recommendations

From this report it can be seen that there is still extreme prejudice and discrimination towards lesbian mothers.

Action is required at all levels if any positive changes are to be made, particularly in relation to lesbian mothers and custody of their children. Given the conservative nature of the judiciary, pressure in changing legal judgments needs to come from those working both inside and outside the area of the law.

Education is needed as well as action if social attitudes towards lesbian mothers are to change. The situation of lesbian mothers is of concern to all women, since any woman can at present be penalised by the law for wanting to control her own sexuality and lifestyle.

What follows are only suggestions of how change could be effected. There is considerably more discussion needed to raise awareness of the issue and to find ways of counteracting discrimination.

THE COURTS

The courts make the prejudiced, unsubstantiated and speculative assumption that lesbianism will have a negative effect on children. At the very least such speculative assumptions should not be allowed to decide custody issues. In some states of the USA there is a requirement on the father's side to produce concrete and factual evidence that the mother's lesbianism is harming the child. This is known as the nexus requirement. It has meant that speculation on future harm (for example the effect of negative community attitudes) is not a basis for deciding custody.

It should not be up to the mother to have to prove her adequacy as a parent merely because she is a lesbian, any more than the father has to prove his adequacy because he is heterosexual. It is up to lawyers in this country to argue for this principle to be established here.

EDUCATION OF LAWYERS

Many lawyers have internalised anti-lesbian attitudes. Often they advise women that they have no hope of getting custody. Lawyers need to be educated on the issues surrounding lesbian custody and to confront their own prejudices towards lesbianism.

WOMEN'S RIGHTS AND THE WELFARE PRINCIPLE

There are no legal guidelines laid down for the interpretation of the welfare principle, although there have been factors established by judges through case law. The primacy of the welfare principle has been 'described' as follows:

> 'It connotes a process whereby, when all the relevant facts, relationships, claims and wishes of parents, risks, choices and other circumstances are taken into account and weighed, the course to be followed will be that which is most in the interests of the child's welfare as the term is now understood' (Lord Justice MacDermott in *J v C*).

This 'description' in fact says nothing about what the welfare of the child means and is therefore wide open to interpretation.

The lack of definition of the welfare principle and the fact that judges have complete discretion in deciding custody issues allow for moralistic and punitive judgements to be made.

We would therefore argue that there should be legal guidelines, laid down by statute, as to the interpretation of the welfare principle. Such guidelines might help to prevent the imposition of judges' own prejudices in deciding custody issues and should minimise the opportunity for a judge to assess a woman's conduct according to his own subjective views of what a 'good mother' should be.

From the beginning of custody law it can be seen that women only acquired custody rights in conjunction with their defined role as mothers. To retain these 'rights' women must comply with the contemporary definition of a good mother. Since 'good motherhood' is male-defined, it is also expected to exist in a situation of subordination and dependence on men. Lesbians in their sexual and emotional independence from men and in their lifestyles do not fit into this role of motherhood. They are therefore rendered 'bad' mothers from whom children need to be protected. In the past a mother's promiscuity or her adultery also rendered her unfit for this role. Also feminists have been defined as 'unfit' mothers. *Thus women's rights to their children are always precarious.*

Women as mothers in general are the only carers of their children and are the most constant figures in their children's lives. In any interpretation of the welfare principle we would argue that this is the most important consideration, and should not be overridden by other considerations except where there is physical ill-treatment, abuse or neglect. The rights of women as parents must be established in law.

CIVIL LIBERTIES

In this context there could be an argument for invoking civil liberties rights for lesbian mothers. The British courts could be in breach of the European Convention on Human Rights in depriving lesbian mothers of custody.

Article 8 states that 'everyone has the right to respect for his(!) private and family life'.

Article 9 states that 'everyone has the right to freedom of thought, conscience and religion'.

Articles 10 and 11 state that everyone has the right to freedom of expression, and freedom of association with others. English courts in imposing conditions on lesbian mothers not to have contact with their lovers or not to go on lesbian or Women's Liberation demonstrations could be breaching Article 11. All these Articles have 'get-out clauses', so that they do not apply where it is a case of 'protecting public health or morals'.

We would argue however that such clauses are not applicable to lesbian custody issues.

FURTHER LEGAL REFORM

Achieving legal reform can be long and difficult. However, in the long term, law reform must be contemplated, and we would see it as the concern of those organisations and individuals who are in a position to do so to take up law reform that would benefit lesbian mothers and their children.

This would include such organisations as the NCCL (National Council for Cicil Liberties), National Council of One Parent Families, The Children's Legal Centre, Family Rights Group, and individual MPs, as well as feminist organisations.

Suggested examples of legal reform

1. Amendment to the Guardianship Act. The words 'regardless of the mother's sexual orientation' could be added to Section 9 of the Guardianship of Minors Act 1971, where it is stated that the court can make an order for custody or access, 'having regard to the welfare of the minor and to the conduct and wishes of the mother and father'.
2. A general anti-discrimination Act which did not allow discrimination on the grounds of sexual orientation might also be of help to lesbian mothers. However, in our view such an act should not be allowed to cover paedophilia.

FOSTERING

Some London boroughs are changing their fostering policy. Fostering does not need the approval of the courts, and in allowing lesbian mothers to foster, social service departments can begin to challenge the prejudiced assumption that lesbians should not be around children.

London local authorities can take a positive lead in ending discrimination against lesbians with children by:

1. Making public statements stating that lesbians should be able to keep custody of their children;
2. Having positive fostering adoption policies for lesbians and
3. Stating in their adoption and fostering publicity that they welcome lesbians as foster or adoptive parents.

CHILDREN OF LESBIAN MOTHERS AND CARE

No child should be taken into care on the grounds that the mother is a lesbian. In fact new DHSS guidelines for Guardians ad Litem[1] (independent people (usually social workers) appointed to look after children's interests in some care cases) specifically state that where a parent is a lesbian this does not mean that their behaviour or lifestyle will have a detrimental effect on the child's welfare, i.e. the mere fact that a child's parent is a lesbian does not qualify as a ground for taking a child into care under the 'moral danger' clause of the Children and Young Persons Act 1969.

Such a statement should be included in any individual guidelines that are issued to social services departments to provide guidance to the 'Care' Acts. Further, social services departments could refuse to carry out supervision of mothers ordered by the courts merely because the mothers are lesbians.

Social service departments and social services committees which make policy must be aware of the anti-lesbian attitudes in their departments and set out to combat this in various ways, including appropriate training for social services staff.

EDUCATING PROBATION OFFICERS AND SOCIAL WORKERS

Anti-lesbian attitudes and beliefs of probation officers who draw up court welfare reports can be instrumental in a lesbian mother's losing custody of her children, as well as reinforcing prejudices of the courts. Where local authority social workers prepare welfare reports, they have similar powers.

Probation officers and social workers need to question their own very basic assumption that being brought up in the heterosexual nuclear family is necessarily what is best for children.

Education needs to begin within their own student (CQSW) and in-service training courses. Educators of these groups might do well to look at the high incidence of sexual abuse of girls within the heterosexual nuclear family and consider the positive alternatives.

Probation officers who already do child custody work should be prepared to discuss their own anti-lesbian and heterosexist attitudes, and adjust them accordingly. Speakers from lesbian mother and/or lesbian groups could be invited to such sessions.

One suggestion from the Australian Royal Commission on homosexual parenting that could be taken up here would be to have lesbian welfare workers brought in, whenever lesbianism appears as an issue in a custody case. Further, within any code of guidance or practice directions for welfare officers it should be stated that the lesbianism of the mother should not be regarded as a negative factor when considering the welfare of the child.

EDUCATION AND SCHOOLS

Education needs to take place at all levels to counteract anti-lesbian attitudes and to allow for the fact that lesbian mothers even exist, from nursery education upwards. Our survey has demonstrated that lesbian mothers are either overtly demonstrated against or felt forced to keep quiet about their lesbianism for fear of discrimination. Schools need to take on board the fact that not all parents of children will be heterosexual and that at least as many as one in ten will be lesbian.

The recognition that a large number of mothers are single parents (one in seven, nationally, and more in many inner city areas of London) has been slow to filter through to the schools. Teachers most frequently address mothers as 'Mrs' and assume that a child lives with both mother and a father, failing to acknowledge different lifestyles.

At a very basic level, lesbian co-parents may not be allowed to collect a child from school, because they do not fit into the school's image of what a parent is.

Books, school materials, and class content do not take into account the existence of lesbian households, or acknowledge that it is a valid lifestyle. Teachers may be responsible for encouraging anti-lesbian attitudes in school students, both in their own attitudes towards lesbianism, and in the content of their lessons and class materials. Where lesbianism is mentioned at all it may be presented as a 'sexual perversion' or a 'medical problem' in sex education and biology classes. Frequently homosexuality may be presented as an entirely male phenomenon, rendering lesbianism once again invisible and establishing female sexuality as entirely passive. In other classes where children look at personal relationships or family life, lesbians may be presented as poor unfortunate misfits who need to be pitied.

Some students are now receiving the currently fashionable 'education for parenthood'. In this context parenthood is only considered viable within marriage. Other forms of parenthood are not generally considered, or, where they are, are presented as forms of parental inadequacy. Adolescents who identify themselves as lesbians are seen as going through a phase and being immature. Therefore they are also viewed as having personality and relationship problems.

The failure of school education to acknowledge lesbianism as a valid and positive identity only encourages negative attitudes in pupils. Of course whilst teachers are under threat of losing their jobs if they come out as lesbians in schools their task is made much more difficult.

In two cases in our survey where teasing of children did take place at school, the school, instead of combatting the attitudes of the pupils, blamed the mother for being a lesbian. In one case the school went so far as to involve social services, which resulted in a care order being made. It is not uncommon in our view that mothers, whether they are lesbian or heterosexual, are blamed for what happens to their children, particularly when children are picked on for being different or for coming from a non-conventional family.[2]

Education Authorities, including the Inner London Education Authority (ILEA), should be prepared to launch training programmes for teachers to combat anti-lesbian and anti-gay attitudes in schools, and also to hold discussions for both students and parents throughout the schools on heterosexism. Teachers should also be able to feel safe enough to come out at school if they wish to without threat of recrimination. Such programmes should be launched in the same way that ILEA conducted and developed their anti-racist policies.

It must be borne in mind that many lesbian mothers suffer from other forms of discrimination; they may be black or working class or disabled or members of an ethnic minority. The idea that lesbians are only white and middle class has also to be combatted in any education programme.

In the long run lesbian mothers and their children should be able to feel comfortable and open about their lifestyles within the school environment.

AID

Some lesbians have children through AID or through self-insemination. However, the recent Warnock Committee Report[3], whilst not specifying that lesbians should be barred access to AID states that 'as a general rule, it is better for children to be born into a two parent family, with both father and mother'.

This assumption is heterosexist and anti-lesbian, as well as negating the experience of the one in seven single mothers in this country. There is no evidence to suppose that it is better for a child to be born to a woman in a heterosexual relationship and in some cases it may be worse.

Contrary to the Warnock Committee Report we would recommend that AID services should be widely available to lesbians and single women who want to have children.

HEALTH

Whilst the 1983 Mental Health Act no longer classifies lesbianism as mental illness, the health professions frequently view it as a 'medical' problem.

This may be particularly apparent to lesbian mothers who are open about their sexuality. Health problems with their children may be blamed in part on the mother's lesbianism. All women who bring their children up without men may be considered at fault by those in the health professions, and lesbians often come in for particular blame.

Health professionals, including health visitors, midwives, nurses and doctors, need to recognise the existence of lesbian mothers who come from all walks of life, and not make the assumption that only heterosexual women have children. Health professionals also must confront their own prejudices and, at a very basic level, cease to regard lesbianism as a source of 'problems'.

The practice in some London boroughs of putting children on the 'at risk' register (a register kept of children thought to be at risk, often including children with non-accidental injuries) because their mothers are lesbians should cease immediately.

Lesbians who have children through AID or self-insemination may experience particular social disapproval and blame if their children have health problems.

Publicity and information in health and mother and baby clinics needs to present images of lesbian families, and recognise generally the existence of other family forms besides the conventional nuclear family. In one particular London borough health visitors refused to have an Under Fives guide in their mother and baby clinics, because it contained some information for lesbian mothers.

HOUSING

From our survey, it was apparent that a small number of women experienced anti-lesbian harassment on housing estates where they lived. Such harassment should entitle the women to priority treatment for rehousing to a 'safe' area by local councils. Further, public housing is still geared to the conventional nuclear family even though it only constitutes one third of all households.

The needs of lesbians who may want to live together with their children should be recognised by housing departments and committees, and lesbian couples should not be discriminated against in favour of heterosexual couples. In the case of the death of the tenant the woman cohabitee/s should not lose their right to the tenancy.

CONCLUSION

Lesbian mothers and our children constitute a sizeable number of families in our society. We experience prejudice, oppression and discrimination – in its most extreme form, by being refused custody of our children. Whilst lesbian mothers have always existed, our visibility, strength, and support for each other and our children are growing. We are here to stay.

The Rights of Women Lesbian Custody Group is part of the campaign to combat oppression and discrimination against lesbian mothers, particularly in relation to child custody and the law.

For further information and what you can do, contact:

ROW Lesbian Custody Group
52/54 Featherstone St
London EC1
Tel: 01 251 6576

SUMMARY OF RECOMMENDATIONS

Legal

1. That the present speculative and prejudiced assumption that lesbianism is or will be harmful to children should not be a basis for deciding custody.
2. That since the above principle will have to be argued mainly by lawyers, lawyers must confront their own anti-lesbian attitudes and prejudices. This should include appropriate training on lesbianism and child custody issues on both law student courses and in-service training courses.
3. That legal guidelines should be introduced for the interpretation of the 'welfare principle' so that the issue of a woman's sexuality and

identify should not be regarded as relevant to the welfare of the child.

4. That women's rights as parents should be established in law, and since women are the main carers of children, this should be the most important consideration in deciding custody issues, rather than male definitions of 'good motherhood'.

5. That in relation to women's rights as parents, the British courts could be in breach of the European convention of Human Rights, since they are limiting these rights. Such a breach should be tested through the European Court.

6. That legal reform be implemented in an amendment to section 9 of the Guardianship of Minors Act 1971 to include a clause which states that a mother's sexuality or identity should not be regarded as a factor in the making of a custody or access order.

7. That a general anti-discrimination Act be introduced that does not allow for discrimination against lesbians and gay men in employment, housing, or other areas of public law.

8. That the Conciliation procedure should not be used as an informal way of deciding lesbian custody disputes.

General

9. That local authorities have positive policies in terms of lesbians being able to adopt and foster children, that they publicise such policies, and that they make statements in support of lesbians caring for and having custody of children.

10. That being a lesbian mother is not a ground for taking a child into care, and that guidelines on the interpretation of the Care Acts are issued accordingly by local authorities.

11. That probation officers and social workers receive appropriate training to combat their own anti-lesbian prejudices and beliefs.

12. That whereever possible welfare reports and social enquiry reports on lesbian mothers should be done by lesbian probation officers and social workers.

13. That Education Authorities implement programmes similar to their anti-racist programmes for teachers, students, and parents, to raise awareness of heterosexism, and combat anti-lesbian and gay

attitudes and practice within the schools and colleges. Lesbian households should be included in school and educational materials.

14. That AID (artificial insemination by donor) should be easily available to lesbians and other single women.

15. That health professionals and health authorities should recognise the existence of lesbian mothers, and cease to view lesbianism as a problem, either to mothers or their children.

16. That health professionals should confront their own anti-lesbian attitudes and practices and appropriate training should be provided for this purpose where necessary. Health publicity and leaflets should include visual images of lesbian families.

17. That anti-lesbian harassment on housing estates should entitle women to priority treatment for re-housing in a 'safe' area, that lesbian households should be recognised as a viable unit for housing, and that lesbian couples should not be discriminated against in favour of heterosexual couples. That where the tenant dies her cohabitee(s) should have a right to the tenancy.

Notes

AN EXPLANATION OF THE CASE REFERENCES IN THE NOTES

For example:
Re K (1977) 1 All ER 647

Re K	This refers to the name of the case
1977	The date of the case
1	The Volume No. of the Law Journal which the case is reported in
All ER	The name of the Law Journal the case is reported in
647	The page the case is reported on

Some of the most common abbreviations used are:

AC	Appeal Court
All ER	All England Law Reports
CH	Chancery
Fam L	Family Law
P	Probate
QB	Queen's Bench
Sol J	Solicitor's Journal
TLR	Times Law Reports
WLR	Weekly Law Reports

CHAPTER 1

1. Two studies on custody and divorce (Susan Maidment, 'A Study in Child Custody' in *Family Law*, Vol. 6 (7), 1976, p. 195–202 and *Family Law*, Vol. 6 (8), 1976, p. 236–41; John Eekelaar et al., *Custody after Divorce: the Disposition of Custody in Divorce Cases in Great Britain*, Centre for Socio-Legal Studies, Oxford, 1977) have shown that a father is more likely to retain custody if, when the divorce petition is filed the child has been living with him and not the mother for some time, whether or not the case is contested.

   Susan Maidment in her pamphlet, 'Child Custody: What Chance for Fathers', National Council for One Parent Families, London, (1981), looking at Appeal cases over five years (1973, 1974, 1977, 1978, 1979) found that there was a slight favouritism (37 per cent) towards mothers with young children where the father's status quo was disturbed, thus upholding the first principle mentioned – that young children should be with their mother, over the second – status quo.
2. *Re K* (1977) 1 All ER 647.
3. *Donchef* (1978) FL 205.
4. In *W v W* (1968) Lord Denning felt it right to be guided by the general principle that a boy aged eight was, all things being equal, better off with his father. However, in a later case, a judge said that this was a mere consideration and not a principle (*Re C an Infant*) (1970) 1 WLR 289.
5. In *S(BD) v S(DJ)* the trial judge gave custody to the 'unimpeachable' father, as he considered it unjust to do otherwise. This approach was condemned by the Court of Appeal (1977) 1 ALL ER 650.
6. *Re D (an Infant)* (1977) 2WLR 79.
7. *Re O (Infants)* Court of Appeal (1962) 1 WLR 724.

CHAPTER 2

1. *E v E* unreported Court of Appeal 27 Nov 1980.

CHAPTER 5

1. *W v W* unreported Court of Appeal 17 June 1980.
   G v D unreported Court of Appeal 16 Feb 1983.
2. *E v E* unreported Court of Appeal 27 Nov 1980.
3. *Belmont v Belmont* no M 16937–74 (NJ Super. Ct., Hunterdon City July 22 1980).
4. *G v D* unreported Court of Appeal 16 Feb 1983.
5. *W v W* unreported Court of Appeal 4 Nov 1976.

CHAPTER 7

1. Insurance policies and proposal forms can be obtained from Partnership Services (Maintenance) Limited, Ludgate House, 107–111 Fleet Street, London EC4A 2AB.
2. The Enduring Powers of Attorney Act 1985.

CHAPTER 11

1. S.M. Cretney, *Principles of Family Law*, Sweet & Maxwell, London, 1979, p.588.
2. *The Guardianship of Minors Act* 1971 repealed the 1886 and 1925 Acts and consolidated their provisions.
3. *Willoughby v Willoughby* 1951 p. 184.
4. *Re L* (Infants) (1962) 3 All ER 4.
5. *Re F* (1969) 2 All ER 766.
6. *B v B* (Court of Appeal) (1975) Family Law (1976) Vol. 6, p. 42.
7. *Re K* (1977) 1 All ER 647.
8. *J v J* (1979) FL 91.

CHAPTER 12

1. Quoted from *Australians At Risk*. Anne Deveson. Sydney. Cassell (1978).

2. Anon., 'A Case of Heads He Wins – Tails She Loses' *Family Law Journal* Vol. 6, 1976, p. 230.
3. Mother's notes taken in court.
4. *W v W* unreported Court of Appeal 3, 4 November 1976.
5. *S v S*, 1 FLR 143 (Court of Appeal 21 June 1978).
6. *Re D (an Infant)* (1977) 2 WLR 79.
7. *W v W* unreported Court of Appeal 17 June 1980.
8. *E v E* unreported Court of Appeal 27 November 1980.
9. *Re P* (a minor), unreported, Court of Appeal 21 July 1982.
10. *G v D, unreported, Court of Appeal 16 February 1983.*
11. Elizabeth Evatt, *A Review of Judgments: (Relevance of and Weight Attached to a Parent's Homosexuality)*, unpublished paper, 1980.
12. Susan Maidment, *Child Custody: What Chance for Fathers*, National Council for One Parent Families, London, 1981.
13. American Humane Association, *Child Protective Services. A National Survey.* ed. Vincent de Francis, Denver, Colo. (1967).
14. London Rape Crisis Report, (1982).

CHAPTER 13

1. In 1819 in the case of Ms Pirie and Ms Woods (two Scottish school teachers, who were accused of lesbianism) it had been argued that upper class British women did not have sexual appetites, and that without a (male) instrument, sexual activity was impossible. The House of Lords accepted these arguments, and the two teachers won their case for libel. See Lillian Faderman, *Surpassing the Love of Men: Romantic Friendship and Love between Women from the Renaissance to the Present.* The Women's Press, London, 1985.
2. Havelock Ellis, *Sexual Inversion,* Macmillan, London, 1897. See also Sonja Ruehl, 'Inverts and Experts, Radclyffe Hall and the Lesbian Identity', in *Feminism, Culture and Politics* edited by Rosalind Brunt and Caroline Rowan, Lawrence & Wishart. (1982).
3. A.C. Kinsey *et al, Female Sexual Response.* Saunders & Co. Phil.

and London (1953).

4. Shere Hite, *The Hite Report. A Study in Female Sexuality.* Dell Publishing Co. USA (1976).

5. See for example *Three Essays on the Theory of Sexuality* (1905). *The Psychogenesis of a Case of Homosexuality in a Woman* (1920) and *Female Sexuality* (1931). In *The standard edition of the complete works of Sigmund Freud* ed. J. Strachey, Hogarth Press; also *Female Sexuality. New Psychoanalytic Views.* Ed. J. Chasseuguet-Smirgel. Virago, London, 1980.

6. Such studies include those done by M. Freedman (1968) 'Homosexuality among Women and Psychological Adjustment.' In D.J. West. *Homosexuality Re-examined,* (Duckworth, London, 1977).

   E. Thompson *et al* 'Personality Adjustment of Male and Female Homosexuals and Heterosexuals' (as above) (1971, 1973).

   M. Wilson and R. Green 'Personality Characteristics of Female Homosexuals' (as above) (1971).

   D.H. Rosen *Lesbians: a Study of Female Homosexuality.* C.C. Thomas, Illinois. (1974).

7. D.J. West. *Homosexuality Re-examined.* Duckworth, London, (1977).

8. Diane Richardson, 'Lesbian Mothers'. In *The Theory and Practice of Homosexuality.* ed. D. Richardson and J. Hart. RKP, London (1981).

9. F.E. Kenyon, 'Homosexuality in the Female'. *British Journal of Hospital Medicine* 3, Vol. 3. (1970). pp. 183–206.

10. M. Freedman, *Homosexuality and Psychological Functioning.* Brooks/Cole Pub. Co. (1971).

    S. Schafer. 'Sociosexual behaviour in Male and Female Homosexuals', *Archives of Sexual Behaviour.* Vol. 6, p. 335 (1977).

11. Bernice Goodman, 'The Lesbian Mother'. *American Journal of Orthopsychiatry*, Vol. 43 (1973) pp. 283–4.

12. Ellen Lewin *et al*, 'Lesbian and Heterosexual Mothers: Continuity and Difference in Family Organisation'. *Paper American Psychological Association.* New York (Sept 1979).

13. Richard L. Rees, 'A Comparison of Children of Lesbian Mothers and Single Heterosexual Mothers on Three Measures of Socialisa-

tion'. *Dissertation Abstracts International.* (1979).

14. Michael Rutter, 'Psychosexual Development' in *Scientific Foundations of Development Psychiatry*, ed. Michael Rutter (Heinemann Medical, London 1980) pp. 322–339.

15. Anon., 'A Case of Heads He Wins – Tails She Loses', *Family Law Journal*, Vol. 6, 1976.

16. Susan Golombok, Ann Spencer, Michael Rutter, 'Children in Lesbian and Single Parent Households: Psychosexual and Psychiatric Appraisal'. Institute of Psychiatry. *Journal of Child Psychology and Psychiatry* Vol. 124 no. 4 (1983) pp. 551–572.

17. Martha Kirkpatrick *et al.*, 'Lesbian mothers and their children. A comparative survey'. *American Journal of Orthopsychiatry*, Vol. 5. no. 3. pp. 545–51. (July 1981).

18. B. Hoeffer, 'Children's Acquisition of Sex-role Behaviour in Lesbian Mother Families', *American Journal of Orthopsychiatry*. pp. 536–544. (1981).

19. Anon., 'A Case of Heads He Wins – Tails She Loses', op. cit.

20. John Money, *Sex Research: New Developments*, Holt, Rinehart & Winston, N.Y., 1965.
    John and Joan Hampson, 'Determinants of Psychosexual Orientation' in F. Beach, ed., *Sex and Behaviour*, John Wiley (1965).

21. Susan Golombok, Ann Spencer, Michael Rutter, 'Children in Lesbian and Single Parent Households', op. cit.

22. Diane Richardson, 'Lesbian Mothers', op. cit.

23. Richard Green, 'Sexual Identity of 37 Children Raised by Homosexual and Transsexual Parents', *American Journal of Psychiatry* 135:6. June, (1978).

CHAPTER 14

1. A.C. Kinsey et al., *Female Sexual Response*, Saunders & Co., Phil. and London (1953).

2. A.P. Bell and Weinberg, *Homosexualities; A Study of Diversity among Men and Women*. Mitchell Beazley, London, (1978).

CHAPTER 15

1. *Bezio v Patenaude* Mass. 410 NE 2d 1207 (1980).
2. *Doe v Doe* 8 Family L. Reporter 2101 (Va. Super. Ct. 1981).
3. *Madeiros v Madeiros* 8 Family L. Reporter 2372 (Vt. Super. Ct. 1982).
4. *Smith v Smith* 5 Family L. Reporter 2450 (Mich. Cir. Ct., Kent Cty. 1979)
5. *MP v SP* N.J. Super. 404A 2d 1256 (1979).
6. *K v K* 2 W.W.R. 462 (1976).
7. *Jacobson v Jacobson* 50 US Law Week 2425 (ND Super. Ct. 1981)
8. *Distefano v Distefano* 60 AD 2d 976 401 NY Supp. 2d 636 (NY Super. Ct. App. Div. 1978).
9. *Re Jane B* 85 Misc. 2d 515, 380 NY Supp. 2d 848 (Super. Ct. 1976)
10. *Loudon v Loudon* D282 246 (Wash. Super. Ct., King Cty. July 1 1971)
11. *Irish v Irish* 300 NW 2d 739 (Mich. Ct. App. 1981), also reported in 7 Family L. Reporter 2256.
12. *L v D 630* SW 2d 240 (Mo. Ct. App. 1982)
13. *Belmont v Belmont* No. M-16937-74 (NJ Super. Ct., Hunterdon Cty. July 22 1980)
14. *Clements v Bennett* 230 Ga 317, 196 S.E. 2d 842 (1973)

CHAPTER 16

(Where cases are unreported only the initials have been given)
1. Family Law Act s.64 1.a.
2. *G* unreported, 21 Nov 1979. Sydney.
3. *T* unreported, 8 Feb 1980. Brisbane.
4. *Campbell v Campbell* 9SASR 25 (1974).
5. *W* unreported, 18 Aug 1978. Adelaide.
6. *In the marriage of Cartwright* FLC 90-302 (1977).
7. *Re P* (a minor) unreported, Court of Appeal 21 July 1982.
8. *Schmidt v Schmidt* FLC 90-685 (1979).
9. Quoted from the judgment of Chief Judge Evatt in the case of *Schmidt v Schmidt* (see above).

10. *P v P* 1976. Victoria. Referred to in PE & RF. The Family Law
     Service Information Bulletin no. 27, p. 3. Butterworths.
11. *In the marriage of Spry* 3 Fam. L.R. 11 330 (1977).
12. *In the marriage of Cartwright*, op. cit.
13. *R* unreported, 26 Oct 1979. Sydney.
14. *Pc & Pr* FLC 90 676 (1979).
15. *T* unreported, 21 Sept 1979. Sydney.

CHAPTER 17

1. Guide for Guardians ad Litem in the Juvenile Court. DHSS 1984.
2. Social Trends 1982. Only 32 per cent of all households are of the
    conventional nuclear family type.
3. Report of the Committee of Inquiry into Human Fertilisation and
    Embryology. Chair Mary Warnock OBE. HMSO July 1984.

Glossary

Access
The right of a parent who does not have care and control of their children to see the children. It may consist of visits or overnight stays. The general rule is that the parent who does not obtain care and control will be given access. Access can be reasonable or defined. Non-parents, e.g. grandparents, are in certain circumstances entitled to apply for access.

Affidavit
A statement in writing and on oath to be used as evidence in court proceedings. The person making it swears it before a solicitor or court official.

Affiliation Order
An order made in the Magistrates' Court which first decides whether or not a man is the child's father; if he is, the court usually orders him to pay maintainance for the child.

AID
Artificial insemination by donor

Anti-lesbianism
1. Attitudes and practices which give lesbianism a negative value;
2. Discrimination against lesbians.

Appellant
Someone who is appealing against a decision of the court.

Barrister
Also known as 'Counsel'. Represents people in court from the Magistrate's Court up to the House of Lords; can only work on the instruction of a solicitor and may only communicate with the client through or in the presence of a solicitor. A barrister works from an office known as 'chambers' together with a group of barristers and organised by one or more 'clerks'. A barrister often specialises in one area of law e.g. family law, commercial law.

Bi-sexual
Someone who relates sexually and emotionally to both sexes.

Care order
Court order giving a local authority most of the parents' legal rights over a child.

Care and control
The day-to-day care of the child. This is nearly always given to one party.

Chambers
Barrister's office

In chambers
Court hearing held in private

Common Law
Judge-made law as it has evolved over the centuries in this country, as distinct from law made by Parliament.

Conciliation
A procedure which has been introduced in order to try to resolve custody disputes without a full court hearing. A Court Welfare Officer is appointed to the case and is supposed to mediate between the parties.

Conference
A meeting between someone who is taking legal action and their barrister. The person's solicitor or representative should be present and the meeting usually takes place in the barrister's office (Chambers).

Consent Order
This is an agreement reached by the parties and approved by the court. Approval is not always automatic. It is an order of the court and is therefore enforceable through the court.

County Court
Deals with non-criminal matters only. It hears domestic violence cases, undefended divorces and related matters of maintainance and custody or access, guardianship (which includes custody disputes between unmarried parents), and adoption.

Court of Appeal
Hears appeals from the High Court and County Court.

Court Welfare Officer
A probation officer, or, in some parts of the country, a local authority social worker, who is appointed by the court to prepare a Welfare Report in cases involving children.

Covenant
Legally binding agreement signed and witnessed. A person can covenant to pay money toward a child's maintainance and get tax relief.

Cross-examination
Questioning of someone in court by the barrister for the other side.

Custody
This is the right to make long-term decisions affecting a child, e.g. on education, health and religion. A parent who has custody has the ultimate legal responsibility for the child, but does not necessarily have

physical care and control over the child. Custody of a child can be held jointly by the parents (joint custody) or by one parent alone (sole custody).

Decree absolute
Court order making a divorce final.

Decree nisi
First part of court order for divorce.

Defined access
Where the court lays down fixed times for access visits.

Deported
Sent out of the country.

Due process
An American term, meaning the right to a fair hearing and the observance of certain principles of justice, outlined in the American Constitution.

Ex-parte
An application to the court by one party to proceedings without the other party having been given notice and therefore not being represented.

Expert witness
An 'expert' witness can give her/his opinion on a subject within her/his expertise (e.g. a psychiatrist). This is an exception to the general rule that witnesses may only speak of facts which they themselves have observed and may not give their opinion on those facts.

Filing at court
Sending legal documents to the court.

Gay
Generally refers to homosexual men, though it is sometimes used to refer to both men and women.

Guardian ad Litem
Is a person appointed by the court from an approved panel of social workers to act as the child's representative (sometimes together with a solicitor) in care proceedings.

Hearsay evidence
Evidence of a fact not actually perceived by a witness with one of her/his own senses, but said by her/him to have been stated by another person. The general rule is that such evidence cannot be used to prove the truth of a fact, but there are exceptions to this rule.

Heterosexism
A belief in the superiority of heterosexuality; policies and practices which serve to elevate heterosexuality and subordinate homosexuality.

Heterosexual
A person who relates sexually and emotionally to the opposite sex.

High Court
Is divided into three divisions. The Family Division deals with defended divorces and can decide on related questions of maintenance, custody and access, guardianship (includes custody disputes between unmarried parents), wardship and adoption.

Homophobia
Fear, dislike, hatred of lesbians and gay men.

Homosexual
A clinical term to describe people who relate sexually and emotionally to the same sex. More often used to refer to gay men.

House of Lords
Hears appeals from the Court of Appeal but only with leave of either the Court of Appeal or the Appeals Committee of the House of Lords.

Illegitimate child
A child who is not born within marriage.

In the closet
Having to keep secret your sexual identity.

Injunction
A court order requiring someone to do, or to stop doing, something.

Interim custody/care and control
This is a temporary order in which custody and/or care and control can be given to any party, pending the final decision on the case.

Irrebuttable presumption
An assumption of the truth of a thing which the law will not allow to be contradicted by any counter-evidence.

Joint custody
Both parents have an equal say in important matters concerning their child/ren after separation/divorce.

Judicial separation
Legal separation of a married couple. The grounds are the same as for a divorce but after a judicial separation the partiess remain legally married.

Judiciary
All judges, magistrates.

Juvenile
A person under the age of 17.

Juvenile Court
See Magistrates' Court.

Law Report
A report of a court decision written up in the officially recognised legal reports, giving the facts of the case/reasons for the decision. Law reports are usually written by barristers.

Law Society
Association of solicitors which also administers Legal Aid.

Leave to Appeal
Permission from the court to lodge an appeal against a decision of the court.

Legal Aid
This is a scheme run by the Law Society and funded by public funds. It enables people whose income and capital do not exceed certain limits to have free legal advice and representation, provided the Law Society is satisfied that they have a case.

Lesbian
Women who relate sexually and emotionally to other women (derived from the Greek Island of Lesbos, where the lesbian poet Sappho had a school in 400 BC).

Magistrates' Court
Deals with criminal (including juvenile) and non-criminal matters. The latter include domestic violence, certain maintenance applications in which the court has power to make orders regarding custody or access, and guardianship (which includes custody disputes between unmarried parents). Sitting as a juvenile court, the magistrates also hear care proceedings.

Maintenance
1. Regular payments of money paid from one spouse (usually the husband) to the other spouse either during or after marriage.
2. Regular payments of money for a child paid by a parent (usually the father).

Matrimonial home
1. House in which wife and husband live;
2. Previously shared home of married couple.

Mediator
A go-between (used in conciliation appointments).

Minor
A person under the age of 18.

Next friend
Adult in whose name legal proceedings are taken on behalf of a child.

Nuclear family
Wife, husband and children living together as a separate group.

Official Solicitor
Acts in High Court cases as the representative of a minor if the court decides that the minor needs independent representation.

Ouster Injunction
Court order directing someone (usually a man) to leave the home.

Party
Someone who is involved in a legal action.

Pathological
Diseased.

Petitioner
Person who applies to the court for a divorce.

Place of Safety Order
A local authority or the police can, without notice to the parents, apply to a magistrate for an order that a juvenile be taken to a place of safety e.g. a local authority children's home or foster-home, for a maximum period of 28 days.

Precedent
A decision made by a previous court which can serve as a rule or pattern to be followed or considered in a subsequent case.

Probation Officer
Person who works in conjunction with the courts and who often writes a report concerning the general welfare of someone coming before the court at the court's request.

Psychiatrist
Someone who studies and treats mental illness.

Psychoanalysis
A method for treating so-called 'mental disorders' by investigating interaction of unconscious and conscious elements of the mind.

Psychologist
Someone who tests and measures mental characteristics.

Psychosexual
A general term often used very loosely by psychologists and psychiatrists to describe a person's identity, development and behaviour, e.g. sex-role behaviour, sexual orientation (lesbian, gay, heterosexual) and gender identity.

On remand
In prison/custody awaiting trial.

Reasonable access
Where access is agreed between the parties without the court laying down specified times. What is reasonable depends on your point of view, and a woman may often be pressurised into agreeing to access arrangements which she finds unreasonable.

Registrar
Sits in the County Court and Family Division of the High Court and is appointed by the Lord Chancellor; deals with procedural issues until the trial of a matter takes place, applications for maintenance and other financial matters in divorce proceedings; deals with access to children where the principle of access is agreed and the only matter in dispute is the amount of access; presides over conciliation appointments where there is a custody dispute.

Reported case
A case decision, which has been written up in the law reports and which therefore can be quoted.

Respondent
Person against whom legal action is being taken.

Rules of natural justice
The right to a fair and unbiased hearing.

SI
Self-insemination.

Solicitor
Can represent people in Magistrates' Courts, County Courts and sometimes in the Crown Court. Rarely represents a client in contested family matters but instead instructs a barrister. A solicitor deals direct with the client and is responsible for the preparation of the case, which includes advising the client, interviewing witnesses and instructing a barrister

Status quo
The current state of affairs; refers here to the current living arrangements of the child.

Statute
Law made by Parliament.

Statutory charge
Charge made by the Law Society for legal costs where property/money is involved.

Supervision Order
A court order which gives the general supervision of a child to a local authority and which can last until the child is 18.

Testamentary guardian
Person named in a will to have custody, care and control of child/ren on a person's death.

Variation Order
Court order changing an original court order.

Ward of Court
A child who has been made a Ward comes under the court's 'protection' i.e. all major decisions relating to the child have to be referred to the court for its approval. The person with whom the child lives has the child's care and control.

Wardship proceedings
Legal action making a child a ward of court.

Welfare Principle
This is contained in S.1. of the Guardianship of Minors Act 1971, which states that the welfare of the child shall be regarded as the first and paramount (i.e. supreme) consideration in any proceedings relating to children.

Welfare Report
A report which may be, and frequently is, ordered by a registrar or judge in any proceedings involving children. It is prepared by a Court Welfare Officer who investigates the circumstances of any person claiming custody or access and interviews the parties and the children. The report has to be shown to the parties to the proceedings.

Further Reading and Information

LESBIAN MOTHERS AND CUSTODY

Our Lives. Lesbian Mothers talk to Lesbian Mothers. Available from Our Lives, c/o Gay Centre, 61 Bloom St, Manchester.
Gillian E Hanscombe and Jackie Forster, eds. *Rocking the Cradle: Lesbian Mothers – a challenge in family living.* Available from Sheba Feminist Publishers, London, 1982.

LEGAL

The Law and Sexuality. Grass Roots Books Ltd. Manchester, 1978.
Gays and the Law by Paul Crane, Pluto Press. 1982.
On Getting Divorced. Consumers' Association, 1983, 14 Buckingham St, London WC2N 6DS.

NATIONALITY AND IMMIGRATION

Women, Immigration and Nationality, by Women, Immigration and Nationality Group. Pluto Press, London, 1985.
Children, Nationality and Immigration, by Kathryn Cronin. Available from The Children's Legal Centre, 20 Compton Terrace, London N1 2UN.
British Nationality, the AGIN Guide, by Ann Dummett with Ian Martin, Action Group on Immigration and Nationality, NCCL, 1984.
The Ins and Outs of Immigration and Nationality Law, by Sue Gray and Anthea Lowe. National Association of Citizens' Advice Bureaux.

GENERAL

Leaving Violent Men. A study of refuges and housing for battered women, 1981. Available from Women's Aid Publications, 116 Portland St, Manchester.

Sexual Violence: The Reality for Women by The London Rape Crisis Centre, The Women's Press, London, (1984).

Outwrite (Monthly feminist newspaper) Oxford House, Derbyshire St, London E1.

Spare Rib (Monthly feminist magazine) 27 Clerkenwell Close, London EC1.

INFORMATION ON CASES

Information on English Appeal cases quoted in this report can be obtained from the ROW office 52/54 Featherstone St, London EC1.

Information on American cases was obtained from the Lesbian Rights Project, 1370 Mission St, 4th Floor, San Francisco, CA 94103.

Lesbian Mother Litigation Manual. Donna J Hitchen JD. 1982, available from the above address.

Lesbian Mothers and their Children: an annotated bibliography of Legal and Psychological Materials. Second Edition (1983). Lesbian Rights Project. San Fransisco. (Thanks to this group for donating this information to the ROW Lesbian Custody Group)

Lambdda Legal Defense and Education Fund, 132 West 43 St, New York, NY 10036.

Further information was obtained from a law student research project *Lesbian Mothers and Child Custody,* 1984, by Varda Bondy, who did a computer search on the Lexis, Dialog, and Eurolex systems.

Information on Australian cases was obtained from material on *Homosexual Parenting* sent to us by Justice Elizabeth Evatt. Chief Judge, Family Court of Australia, Sydney. This material included *A Review of Judgments: (Relevance of and weight attached to a parent's homosexuality.)* Elizabeth Evatt C.J.

Homosexuality of Parent: A New Issue in Custody Dispute. 5 Monash
UL Review 305 (1979).
(Other papers unpublished.)

PSYCHOLOGICAL AND STATISTICAL MATERIALS

Some materials are also listed under the reference section for specific
chapters (e.g. Chapter 4 'The Myths'). These materials may be used to
counteract certain heterosexist assumptions and myths, which may be
raised by the courts or other institutions. However they frequently
start from the premise that lesbians have to prove their adequacy as
mothers and make other heterosexist and anti-lesbian assumptions.
The views expressed in the studies quoted therefore do not necessarily
reflect the views of the ROW Lesbian Custody Group.

*Studies which counteract beliefs about the effect of lesbian
households on children*

'Children in Lesbian and Single Parent Households:Psychosexual and
Psychiatric Appraisal.' Susan Golombok, Ann Spencer, Michael
Rutter. Institute of Psychiatry, *Journal of Child Psychology and
Psychiatry* Vol. 24, no. 4 (1983). pp.551–72. Looks at emotional
development, peer group relationships, psychosexual development of
children including sex role behaviour, direction of children's sexual
interest, children's adult contacts, and a number of other factors.
Compares 37 children from lesbian households with 38 children from
single heterosexual households. No significant difference found
between the two groups.

'Lesbian Mothers and their Children. A comparative survey'. Martha
Kirkpatrick, M. Smith, R. Roy (1981). *American Journal of Orthopsychiatry* Vol 5, no. 13 pp. 545–51. Compares 20 children of both sexes
with equal numbers of children of single heterosexual mothers. Gender
development of the children not identifiably different in the two
groups.

'Sexual Identity of 37 Children Raised by Homosexual or Transvestite
Parents'. Richard Green. *American Journal of Psychiatry* 135.6 (June

1978). Looks specifically at the teasing issue. Found no prevalent teasing of lesbian mothers' children; where there was children could cope with it adequately. Also did not use a control group, so could not predict whether teasing was any higher than for heterosexual children. 'Children's Acquisition of Sex Role Behaviour in Lesbian-Mother Families'. B. Hoeffer. *American Journal Orthopsychiatry*. Vol 51.3. (1981). Looked at sex-role traits and behaviours using Blocks Toy Preference test on children of lesbian mothers and children of single heterosexual mothers. No significant difference between the two groups. Research hypothesised that children's peers have greatest influence on sex role development.

Mothering patterns

The following studies show no difference in mothering patterns between lesbian mothers and single heterosexual mothers.

A Comparison of Children of Lesbian and Single Heterosexual Mothers on three measures of socialisation. Richard L. Rees (1979). Compared 12 children of heterosexual single and 12 lesbian mothers. Findings indicated no significant difference in parenting style.

'Lesbianism and Motherhood Implications for Child Custody'. Ellen Lewin. *Human Organisation*. Vol.40, no.1. (1981).
also:

'Lesbian and Single Heterosexual Mothers; Continuity and Difference in Family Organisation'. E. Lewin, Lyons and Terrie, *Paper American Psychological Ass*. New York (Sept 1979). Findings indicated significant similarity in the way mothers met the challenge of daily life and in the perceptions of being a single mother. Latter study found increased stress put on lesbian mothers through fear of loss of custody.

'The Lesbian Mother'. Bernice Goodman. *American Journal of Orthopsychiatry* Vol. 43, pp.283–4 (1973). Compared participants of heterosexual mothers' group, and lesbian mothers' group over two year period. Found that similarities of motherhood far exceeded differences.

The above studies in general indicate:

1. No evidence of pathology in children of lesbians.

2. No evidence of confusion in gender or sexual identity among children of lesbians, or difference in sexual interests of children of lesbian mothers and heterosexual mothers.
3. No significant difference between children of lesbians and children of heterosexual mothers in overall emotional adjustment.
4. No significant difference in peer group relationships and children's friendships. No negative impact from social stigmatisation, depending on mother's level of adjustment to her situation.
5. No significant difference in the level of ability of mothering between lesbian mothers and single heterosexual mothers.
6. No significant difference in concern over children's development.

Lesbian identity and personality

The following studies show that lesbians are in fact better adjusted and less neurotic than heterosexual women:

'Personality Characteristics of Female Homosexuals'. M. Wilson and R. Green, *American Psychological Reports* Vol. 28, pp. 407–12 (1971).

'Adjustment of Homosexual and Heterosexual Women'. *British Journal of Psychiatry*. Vol. 120.

'Adjustment of Homosexual and Heterosexual Women'. Marian Siegleman, *British Journal of Psychiatry*. Vol. 120, p. 477–81 1972.

See also:

Homosexuality Re-examined. D.J. West. Duckworth (1977), for a number of studies on this aspect.

Lesbian relationships, stability, instability, etc.

The following studies show that lesbian relationships have little in common with male homosexuality and that lesbians do not tend to differ from heterosexual women in patterns of monogamy and non-monogamy.

'Homosexuality in the Female'. F.E. Kenyon. *British Journal of Hospital Medicine* (1970).

'Sociosexual Behaviour in Male and Female Homosexuals'. S. Schafer. Shows that being a woman tends to influence sexual behaviour and

relationships of lesbians to a greater extent than being 'homosexual'.
Archives of Sexual Behaviour Vol. 6, p. 355 (1977).
Homosexuality and Psychological Functioning. M. Freedman Brooks/
Cole Publishing Co. (1971).

General

Lesbians, Women and Society. E.M. Ettore, RKP (1980). Demon-
strates social and political identity of lesbianism.
The Theory and Practice of Homosexuality. D. Richardson, J. Hart.
Chapter 8 'Lesbian Mothers' (1981).
Homosexualities: a Study of Diversity among Men and Women. A.P.
Bell and Weinburg, London. Mitchell Beazley (1978). (One of the few
studies which did not use an all-white sample.)

Education

'Homophobia and Education', *Interracial Books for Children Bulletin*
Vol. 14, nos. 3 and 4 1983, 1841 Broadway, New York, NY 10023.
Girls are Powerful. Young Womens' Writings. ed. Susan Hemmings.
Sheba Feminist Publishers (1982).

Statistics

Social Trends (1982). Only 32 per cent of all households consist of
'conventional' nuclear families. General Register Office 1966 statistics
demonstrated that the 'conventional' nuclear family i.e. nuclear
families of married couples and one or more child, comprised only four
out of ten British households. The existence of the conventional family
is thus a myth. (General Register Office 1966: Table 1.)
See also *Conventional Families.* Ann Oakley in *Families in Britain,* ed.
R.N. Rapoport, M.P. Fogarty, and R. Rapoport. RKP (1982).

Child abuse statistics can be found in the only study which has looked
at sexual orientation of sex offenders.
*Child Protective Services. A National Survey. Sexual Abuse of
Children,* ed. Vincent de Francis. American Humane Association.

Denver, Colorado. (1967). Found that ·97 per cent of child sexual abusers were male heterosexuals.

Female Sexual Response Kinsey *et al.* (1953) Still provides the only reliable statistics on *estimates* of the number of lesbians. Since Kinsey there have been no large scale studies done which are not self-selected. Since the growth of the lesbian and women's liberation movements which have challenged the basis of heterosexuality as the 'normal' state numbers may be much higher than Kinsey's estimate of one in ten. Bell and Weinburg (1978) (see above) in their large-scale study on lesbians and gay men found that one in five of their lesbian sample had children whereas only one in ten of the homosexual men did.

Other reports

Report from Older Lesbians Conference (1984). Has useful section on heterosexism and family life, and makes recommendations. Available from OLN c/o London Friend, 274 Upper St. London N1.
Something to tell you . . . the Experiences and Needs of Young Lesbians and Gay Men in London. London and Gay Teenage Group (1984). Available from Research Project. BM LGTG, London WC1 3XX.

Information on law reports

Law reports are published reports of the decisions of courts and tribunals and the reasons given for the decisions. They are usually written by barristers.

Where to find Law Reports

As has already been stated there are very few cases concerning lesbian mothers written up in the law reports. However, just in case there are any in the future, the following information may be relevant.

The two main reports are the All England Law Reports (All ER) and Weekly Law Reports (WLR). There are also Law Reports, Appeal Cases, (AC) and Family Law Reports, which may be most relevant for looking for lesbian custody cases. Most law reports are issued yearly. *The Times* newspaper also gives reports on legal decisions, and the courts regard these reports as 'official' and they can therefore be quoted.

Law reports are not easily available. Some central libraries have them in their reference sections. Some areas have law libraries run by their local Law Societies. Otherwise university or polytechnic libraries may have them, particularly if they run law courses. Many solicitors and Law Centres have at least some law reports.

CONTACT LIST

(This is not a comprehensive list. For local lesbian groups and centres phone London Lesbian Line: 01 251 6911. Also see Resources at the end of each chapter.)

Legal

Rights of Women Lesbian Custody Group, for solicitors experienced in doing lesbian custody cases, information and speakers on lesbian custody. Tel: 01 251 6576. Daytime only.
Action for Lesbian Parents (National) c/o The Corner Bookshop, 162 Woodhouse Lane, Leeds LS2 9H8. For help and information.
Lesbian Mother groups for support/custody/action, local and all London groups phone London Lesbian Line Tel: 01 251 6911. Mondays and Fridays 2-10 pm. Tuesday, Wednesday, Thursday 7-10 pm.

Lesbian groups

Black Lesbian Support Network Black Women's Centre, 41a Stockwell Green, London SW9.
Working Class Lesbian Group c/o A Woman's Place, Hungerford House, Victoria Embankment, London WC1.
Jewish Lesbian Group c/o A Woman's Place (see above).
Older Lesbians Network c/o London Friend, 274 Upper St, London N1. Tel: 01 354-1846 after 7 pm, Thursdays. Has support network for

older lesbians with teenage children.

Lesbian and Policing Project (LESPOP) offers support and advice to lesbians having dealings with the police, and in investigating all aspects of the policing of lesbians in London. 38 Mount Pleasant, London WC1X 0AP. Tel: 01 833 4996.

Lesbian Employment Rights supports lesbians where discrimination at work is taking place, and campaigns against anti-lesbian discrimination in un/employment. Room 205, Southbank House, Black Prince Road, London SE1 7SJ. Tel: 01 587 1636.

GEMMA a self help group of lesbians with/without disabilities. BM Box 5700, London WC1N 3XX. Enquiries welcome in braille or on cassette.

Young Lesbians Group Tel: 01 263 5932. Mondays 7.30–10 pm.

Lesbians at London Friend 274 Upper St, London N1. Telephone line and social group 354 1846. Thursdays only 7.30–10 pm.

KENRIC 'non-political' social group for lesbians in London. BM Kenric, London WC1N 3XX.

Catholic Lesbian Sisterhood, BM Reconciliation, London WC1N 3XX.

Phone lines

London Lesbian Line Tel: 01 251 6911 (for times see above).

London Friend Tel: 01 354 1846. Lesbians only Thursday 7.30–10 pm.

Gay Switchboard (Mixed) 24 hour service. 01 837 7324.

A Woman's Place, Hungerford House, Victoria Embankment, London WC2. Tel: 01 836 6081.

Brixton Black Women's Centre, 41A Stockwell Green, London SW9.

Asian Women's Resource Centre 134 Minet Ave, London NW10. Tel: 01 961 6549.

Women's Aid London Tel: 01 251 6538/7 (offers refuge for women and children forced to leave home because of violence from the man they live with).

Women's Aid Northern Office 061 228 1069.

Scottish Women's Aid: Edinburgh 031 668 2949; Glasgow 041 248 2989.

Northern Ireland Women's Aid 0232 24904.

Republic of Ireland 0001 961 002.
London Rape Crisis Centre open 24 hours. Tel: 01 837 1600. PO Box 69, London WC1X 9NJ.

Legal general

Law centres offer general advice on immigration and welfare rights. Phone Law Centres' Federation for your local centre. Tel: 01 387 8570. 164 North Gower St, London NW1.
Rights of Women phone-line legal advice sessions Tuesdays, Wednesdays and Thursdays 7 pm–9 pm. Tel: 01 251 6577.
Family Rights Group 6–9 Manor Gardens, Holloway Rd, London N7. (For rights of parents with children in care.)

Index

The Women's Press is a feminist publishing house. We aim to publish a wide range of lively, provocative books by women, chiefly in the areas of fiction, literary and art history, physical and mental health and politics.

To receive our complete list of titles, send a stamped addressed envelope. We can supply books direct to readers. Orders must be pre-paid with 60p added per title for postage and packing. We do, however, prefer you to support our efforts to have our books available in all bookshops.

The Women's Press, 34 Great Sutton Street, London EC1V 0DX

Lillian Faderman
Surpassing the Love of Men

*Romantic Friendship and Love between
Women from the Renaissance to the Present*

'A fascination from beginning to end . . . a sort of revelation'
Jill Tweedie, *The Guardian*

A quietly revolutionary book which reconstructs a lost history of
women loving women. Here Lillian Faderman explores the
different forms that love has taken over the years, from the
elaborate deceptions practised by Deborah Sampson, soldier of
the American Revolution, to the genteel Ladies of Llangollen and
the notorious 'Boston marriages' of the nineteenth century.

Dr Faderman is a full professor at California State University, San
Francisco.

Fully illustrated

Social History/Women's Studies
0 7043 3977 3   £6.95

Jan Bradshaw & Mary Hemming, editors
Girls Next Door

Lesbian feminist stories
Introduced by Alison Hennegan

Eleanor discovers an unexpected love affair in her late aunt's letters. Kira, a lesbian from another planet, pays a visit to Earth. Speculation abounds when a neighbour discovers Miss Jones and Miss Evans naked in their sitting room ...

Witty, touching, funny, sad, some by established writers and others by new, all these stories reflect the warmth and comfort of the feeling of women for each other ...

First world publication

Fiction
0 7043 3980 3   £3.95
0 7043 2871 2 (hardcover)   £7.95

Caeia March
Three Ply Yarn

'The blitz on the London docks got my mum. My dad died in Burma. That's when Dora and me first took to cuddling. Behind the hay barn, while Nellie collected eggs.'

This passionate story is narrated by three women, Dee, Lotte and Esther, as they struggle to take command of their own lives in a world they have not made.

The three choose different paths. Lotte marries for money, Esther seeks education and politics, Dee loves women and learns, through her relationship with her lover's black daughter, about an oppression different from her own. Yet their lives increasingly intertwine, and their realisation grows of the importance of other women to each of them.

Full of the realities of working-class lesbian experience, *Three Ply Yarn* is an absorbing read from an important new writer.

An original publication from The Women's Press

Fiction
0 7043 4007 0   £3.95
0 7043 5003 3 (hardcover)   £8.95

Suniti Namjoshi
The Conversations of Cow

Suniti and Bhadravati disagree about almost everything – which is
hardly surprising as Suniti is an average middle of the road lesbian
separatist and Bhadravati is a Brahmin lesbian cow, goddess of a
thousand faces and a thousand manifestations.

Suniti has been unlucky in love and thinks she is becoming a
misogynist. So it's only natural that when Bhadravati transforms
herself into a woman, Suniti decides to become a goldfish (or
perhaps a poodle or another cow). When Bhadravati manifests
herself as a man, things can only get worse.

First world publication

Fiction
0 7043 3979 X   £2.95
0 7043 2870 4 (hardcover)   £7.95

Anna Livia
Accommodation Offered

' "There is a woman in Stockwell sinning," insisted Quercus.
"What's her sin?"
"Despair," said Quercus squeamishly.
"She has been ironing now for three hours, satin sheets of oyster
cream . . ." '

When Polly advertises two vacant rooms in her South London
home, Kim and Sadie move in: bus conductor Kim, and awkward,
gangling Sadie. Tensions develop as the differences between the
three women, their diverse backgrounds and politics as lesbians,
begin to divide them. Fortunately the household is watched over
by the Liberty Boddesses of Hortus, prepared to risk even divine
censure and banishment if they can help . . .

As all who enjoyed her first novel, *Relatively Norma*, will know,
Anna Livia's is a unique voice and her style a special blend of
humour and seriousness.

An original publication from The Women's Press

Fiction
0 7043 3951 X   £3.95
0 7043 2857 7 (hardcover)   £7.95

The Women's Press Handbook Series
The London Rape Crisis Centre
Sexual Violence
A Reality for Women

Written by three members of the London
Rape Crisis Centre Collective, this handbook
draws on the experience and analysis of the
Centre to discuss the politics of rape and its
use as a form of social control, as well as
offering full practical information about the
medical and legal aspects, and the emotional
reactions of the woman involved, her friends
and family.

Addressed to women who have been raped,
and those who are involved as supporters, as
medical and legal advisers, *Sexual Violence* will
prove invaluable to professionals such as
social workers, policewomen, policemen and
doctors, as well as to all women who have
been, or may ever be, raped: either in the
legal definition of the word, or through
sexual harassment, which the authors define
as itself a form of rape.

Health/Women's Studies
0 7043 3910 2   £3.50